CONCEPT OF SCIENCE-TERM 2

CBSE BOARD TERM-2 NOTES

AADIL KHAN

ISBN 979-888569796-5

My Parents & My Teachers
who worked hard to give me the

Best of life & learning.

Contents

Preface

Dear Reader,

This book covers the syllabus of CBSE & State Board like Rajasthan Board, MP Board etc. & other courses related to Secondary Classes by various Boards. This book contains numerous solved MCQ, CBSE Board Questions & Concept Classes Sample Papers with wide variety of figures and tables.

The content of book is developed in very easier way & written in lucid manner.

At the end of each Chapter, some Review Questions have been added for the students to check understanding of the subject matter.

In spite of our best efforts, some errors might do creep in while writing & publishing book. We will be highly grateful if errors are bought to our notice.

For your constructive criticism & feedback, feel free to mail at: conceptclassesjpr@gmail.com

Dispute, if any, shall be subject to Jaipur Jurisdiction only.

ACKNOWLEDGEMENTS

"*I would like to thank my* ***parents & wife*** *who give me support for every moment of life. This book is dedicated to all my friends for their encouragement, insightful comments & hard questions.*

Besides my parents, wife & friends, I would like to thank all my students."

I

Carbon and its compounds

Chapter-4

Carbon: Introduction

Atomic Number: 6
Electronic configuration: 2, 4
Valence electrons: 4
Property: Non-metal

Abundance: Carbon is the 4th most abundant substance in-universe and 15th most abundant substance in the earth's crust.

Compounds having carbon atoms among the components are known as carbon compounds. Previously, carbon compounds could only be obtained from a living source; hence they are also known as organic compounds.

Bonding In Carbon: Covalent Bond

The bond formed by sharing of electrons is called a covalent bond. Two or more atoms share electrons to make their configuration stable. In this type of bond, all the atoms have similar rights over shared electrons. Compounds that are formed because of covalent bonds are called COVALENT COMPOUNDS.

Covalent bonds are of three types: Single, double, and triple covalent bonds.

Physical Properties of Covalent Compounds

→ Covalent compounds have low melting and boiling points as they have weak intermolecular force.

→ They are generally poor conductor of electricity as electrons are shared between atoms and no charged particles are formed.

Versatile Nature of Carbon

The two characteristic properties of carbon element which lead to the formation of large number of compounds :

- Catenation: Carbon can link with carbon atoms by means of covalent bonds to form long chains, branched chains and closed ring. Compound Carbon atoms may be linked by single, double or triple bonds.
- Tetravalency: Carbon has 4 valence electrons. Carbon can bond with four carbon atoms, monovalent atoms, oxygen, nitrogen and sulphur.

Hydrocarbon

→ Compounds made up of hydrogen and carbon are called hydrocarbon.

→ There are two types of Hydrocarbons.

(i) Saturated Hydrocarbons

(ii) Unsaturated Hydrocarbons

Saturated Hydrocarbons

Single bond between carbon atoms.

—C—C—

Alkanes are saturated hydrocarbons.

General Formula: C_nH_{2n+2}

Unsaturated Hydrocarbons

Double or triple bond between carbon atoms. Alkenes and Alkynes are unsaturated hydrocarbons.

Alkenes: —C=C—

General formula: C_nH_{2n}

Alkynes: —C≡C—

General Formula: CnH_{2n-2}

Electron Dot Structure of Saturated Hydrocarbons

- Ethane C2H6

• Ethane C_2H_6

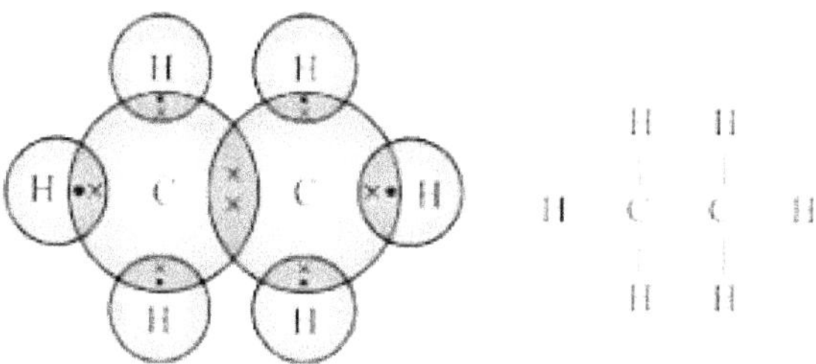

Names, molecular formulae, and structure formulae of saturated hydrocarbons (Alkanes):

No. of C atoms	Name	Formula	Structure
1	Methane	CH_4	H H-C-H H
2	Ethane	C_2H_6	H H H-C-C-H H H
3	Propane	C_3H_8	H H H H-C-C-C-H H H H
4	Butane	C_4H_{10}	H H H H H-C-C-C-C-H H H H H
5	Pentane	C_5H_{12}	H H H H H H-C-C-C-C-C-H H H H H H
6	Hexane	C_6H_{14}	H H H H H H H-C-C-C-C-C-C-H H H H H H H

Source- NCERT BOOK

Electron-Dot Structure :

Ethane C_2H_6

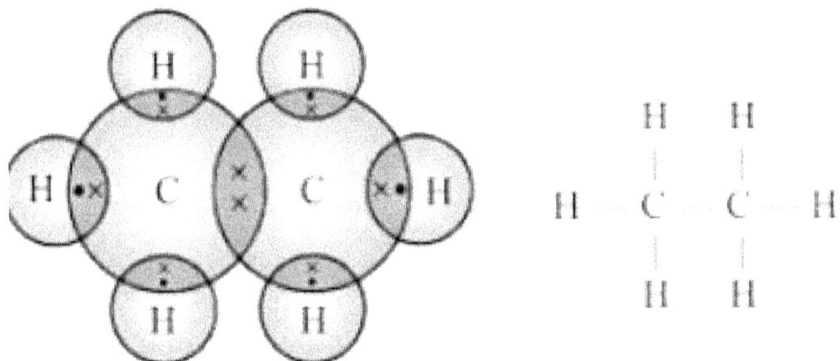

- Ethene (C_2H_4)

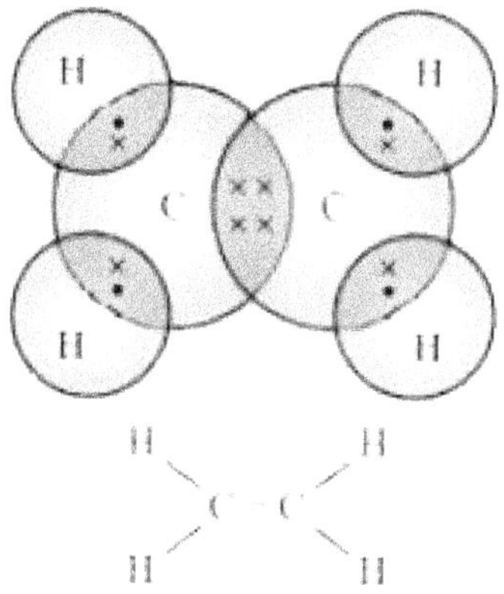

- Ethyne (C_2H_2)

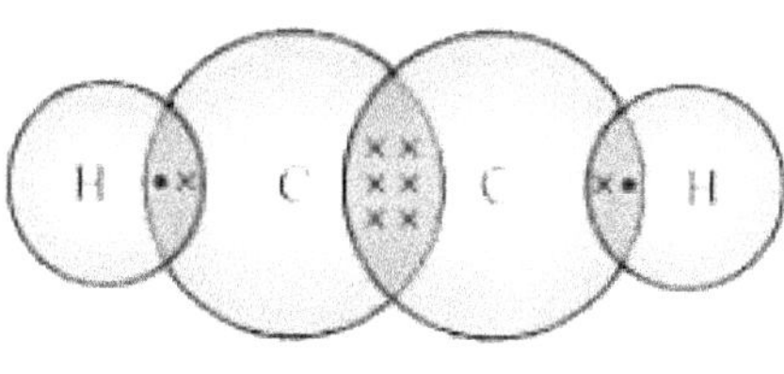

$H-C\equiv C-H$

Carbon Compounds on the Basis of Structure :

Name of Hydrocarbon	Mileculas formula	Structural Formula
Alkenes :		
1. Ethene	C_2H_4	 H H H — C = C — H
2. Propene	C_3H_6	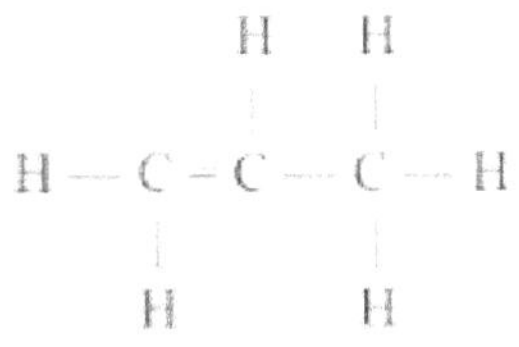 H H H — C – C — C — H H H
3. Butane	C_4H_8	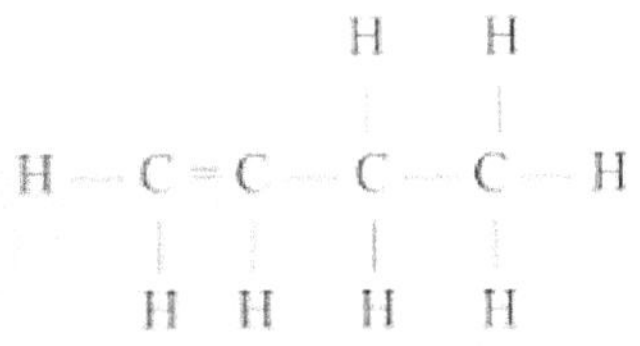 H H H — C = C — C — C — H H H H H
Alkynes :		
1. Ethyne	C_2H_2	H — C ≡ C — H
2. Propyne	C_3H_4	 H H — C ≡ C — C — H H
3. Butyne	C_4H_6	 H H H — C ≡ C — C — C — H H H

Cyclic Structure :

(a) (b)

Structure of cyclohexane (a) carbon skeleton (b) complete molecule

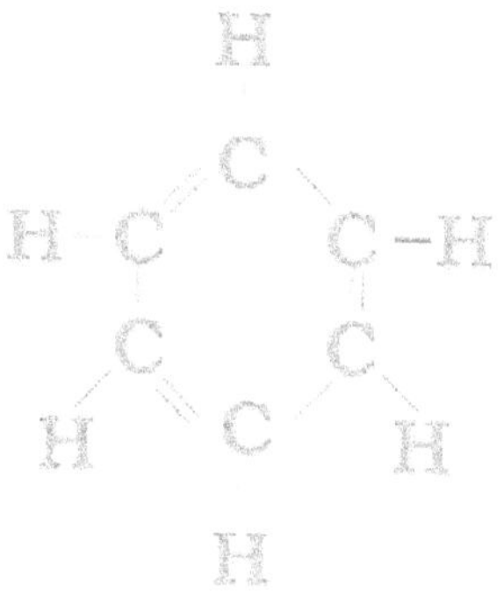

Structure of Benzene C_6H_6

Functional Groups

In the hydrocarbon chain, one or more hydrogen atoms is replaced by other atoms in accordance with their valancies. These are heteroatom.

These heteroatoms or groups of atoms that make carbon compounds reactive and decide their properties are called functional groups.

Hetero atom	Functional group	Formula of functional group
Cl/Br	Halo- (Chloro/bromo)	—Cl, —Br (substitutes for hydrogen atom)
Oxygen	1. Alcohol	—OH
	2. Aldehyde	$-C(=O)H$
	3. Ketone	$-C(=O)-$
	4. Carboxylic acid	$-C(=O)-OH$

Functional Groups

Homologous Series

It is a series of compounds in which some functional group substitutes for the hydrogen in a carbon chain.

Example: Alcohols – CH_3OH, C_2H_5OH, C_3H_7OH, C_4H_9OH

• They have the same general formula.

They have the same chemical properties but show a gradual changes in physical properties.

Nomenclature of Carbon Compounds

(i) Identify the number of carbon atoms in compounds.

(ii) Functional group is indicated by suffix or prefix*.

*Please Prefer NCERT BOOK Table

Chemical Properties of Carbon Compounds

Combustion Reaction: Carbon and carbon compounds give carbon dioxide, vapor, heat, and light on burning in air. Following are some of the examples of combustion reactions of organic compounds:

$C + O_2 \Rightarrow CO_2 + Heat + Light$

$CH_4 + 2O_2 \Rightarrow CO_2 + 2H_2O + Heat + Light$

$CH_3C_2OH + O_2 \Rightarrow CO_2 + H_2O + Heat + Light$

Oxidation:

In a combustion reaction, carbon compounds are oxidized in the presence of oxygen. The following example is different because alkaline KMn04 is the oxidizing agent in this reaction.

$CH_3CH_2OH + (Alkaline\ KMnO_4/Acidified\ K_2Cr_2O_7) \Rightarrow CH_3COOH$

Addition Reaction:

The formation of larger molecules by the addition of more radicals is known as the addition reaction. For example; ethene is converted into ethane when heated with the catalyst nickel.

$CH_2=CH_2 + H_2 + (Nickel\ catalyst) \Rightarrow CH_3\text{-}CH_3$

When ethene undergoes an additional reaction with chlorine, it gives dichloroethane.

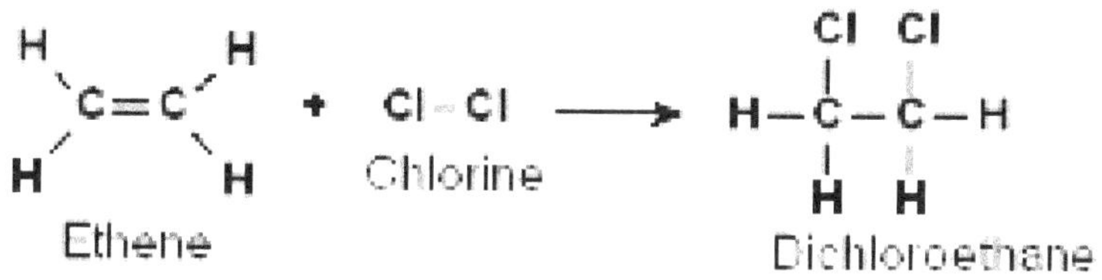

Substitution Reaction:

Replacement of a functional group or any atom by another atom or functional group is known as substitution reaction. Substitution reactions are single displacement reactions.

When methane reacts with chlorine gas in the presence of sunlight, it gives chloromethane and hydrogen chloride.

$CH_4 + Cl_2 + Sunlight \Rightarrow CH_3Cl + HCl$

Similarly, ethane gives chloroethane when it reacts with chlorine in the presence of sunlight.

$C_2H_6 + Cl_2 + Sunlight \Rightarrow C_2H_5Cl + HCl$

Some Important Organic Compounds

Ethanol (C_2H_5OH)

- Ethanol is commonly known as alcohol and spirit.
- The general name of ethanol is ethyl alcohol.
- Ethanol is the main constituent of all alcoholic drinks
- Ethanol is soluble in water
- Ethanol is a very good solvent
- Ethanol is used in the manufacturing of medicines, such as tincture iodine, cough syrup, etc.
- Taking even a small quantity of pure ethanol may prove lethal
- Taking dilute ethyl alcohol can cause drunkenness

Reaction of ethanol with sodium metal:

When ethanol reacts with sodium, it gives sodium ethoxide and hydrogen gas.

$2CH_3CH_2OH + 2Na \Rightarrow 2CH_3CH_2ONa + H_2$

Oxidation of ethanol: Ethanol gives ethanoic acid on oxidation.

$CH_3CH_2OH + (Alkaline\ KMnO_4/Acidified\ K_2Cr_2O_7) \Rightarrow CH_3COOH$

Dehydration of ethanol: Ethanol gives ethene and water when it is heated with concentrated sulphuric acid.

$CH_3CH_2OH + Conc.\ H_2SO_4 \Rightarrow CH_2{=}CH_2 + H_2O$

Ethanoic Acid (CH_3COOH)

The structural formula of ethanoic acid is as follows:

```
     H   O
     |   ||
 H — C — C — O — H
     |
     H
```

- The general name of ethanoic acid is acetic acid.
- The melting point of ethanoic acid is 290K.
- Ethanoic acid freezes in winter and hence it is also known as glacial acetic acid.
- Ethanoic acid is a colorless liquid.
- 5% to 8% solution of acetic acid in water is known as vinegar.

- Vinegar is used as a preservative in pickles.
- Carboxylic acids are weak acids compared to mineral acids.

The reaction of ethanoic acid with base: Ethanoic acid gives sodium acetate when it reacts with sodium hydroxide.

$CH_3COOH + NaOH \Rightarrow CH_3COONa + H_2O$

Esterification of ethanoic acid: Ethanoic acid gives ethyl acetate when it reacts with ethanol in presence of conc. sulphuric acid. This reaction is called the esterification reaction.

$CH_3COOH + C_2H_5OH \Rightarrow CH_3COOC_2H_5 + H_2O$

The IUPAC name of Ethyl acetate is Ethyl Ethanoate. Ethyl acetate is also known as an ester. Ester is a sweet-smelling compound. It is used in making perfumes and as a flavoring agent. When ethyl ethanoate reacts with a base or acid, it gives back ethanol and ethanoic acid.

$CH_3COOC_2H_5 + NaOH \Rightarrow CH_3COOH + C_2H_5OH$

Saponification: Ester of higher fatty acids gives sodium salt of higher fatty acid; when heated with glycerol and sodium hydroxide. Sodium salts of higher fatty acids are known as soaps. This reaction is called saponification (soap-making).

The reaction of ethanoic acid with sodium carbonate and sodium bicarbonate:

Ethanoic acid gives sodium acetate, water, and carbon dioxide when reacts with sodium carbonate or sodium bicarbonate (sodium hydrogen carbonate).

$2CH_3COOH + Na_2CO_3 \Rightarrow 2CH_3COONa + CO_2 + H_2O$

$CH_3COOH + NaHCO_3 \Rightarrow CH_3COONa + CO_2 + H_2O$

Soaps and Detergents:

Soap: Ester of higher fatty acids is called soap. It is manufactured by the reaction of easter of higher fatty acid with sodium hydroxide. The sodium salt so formed has cleansing property. This reaction is called saponification since it is used in making soap.

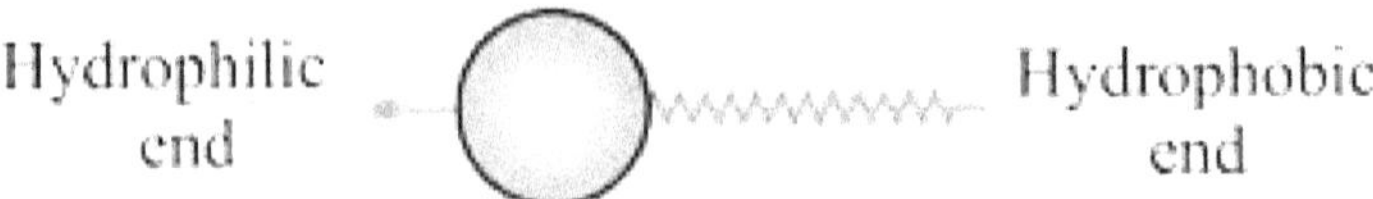

Structure of soap molecule

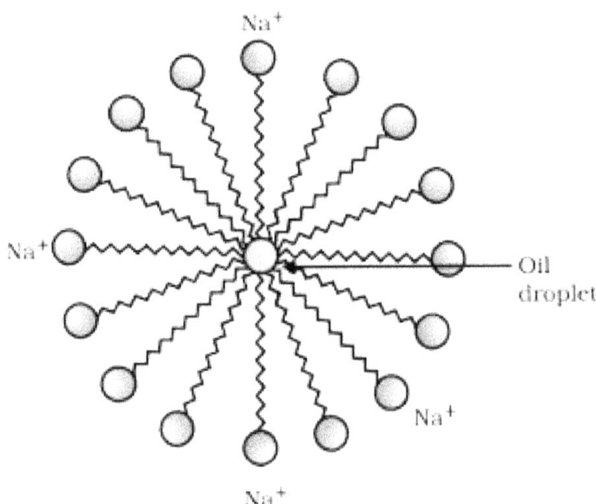

Formation of micelles

Detergent: Soap cannot form lather in hard water. To overcome this problem, detergents were introduced. Detergent is also known as soapless soap. Detergent is sodium salt of benzene sulphonic acid or sodium salt of long-chain alkyl hydrogen sulphate.

The cleansing action of soap:

A soap molecule has two ends. One end is hydrophilic and another end is hydrophobic. In other words, one end is lipophobic (hydrophilic) and another end is lipophilic (hydrophobic). When soap is dissolved in water and clothes are put in the soapy solution, soap molecules converge in a typical fashion to make a structure; called a micelle. The hydrophobic ends of different molecules surround a particle of grease and make the micelle; which is a spherical structure. In this, the hydrophilic end is outside the sphere and the hydrophobic end is towards the center of the sphere. That is how soap molecules wash away dirt and grease by making micelles around them.

Soap and Hard Water: Hard water often contains salts of calcium and magnesium. Soap molecules react with the salts of calcium and magnesium and form a precipitate. This precipitate begins floating as an off-white layer over water. This layer is called scum. Soaps lose their cleansing property in hard water because of the formation of scum. Detergents are used; instead of soaps; in hard water to overcome the problem. Detergents are usually ammonium or sulphonate salts of carboxylic acids. The charged ends of these compounds do not form a precipitate with calcium or magnesium salts in hard water. Hence, detergents retain their cleansing property in hard water.

The magnesium and calcium salt present in hard water react with soap molecules to form an insoluble product called scum. This scum creates difficulty in cleansing action.

· By use of detergent, insoluble scum is not formed with hard water and cloths get cleaned effectively

Flowchart

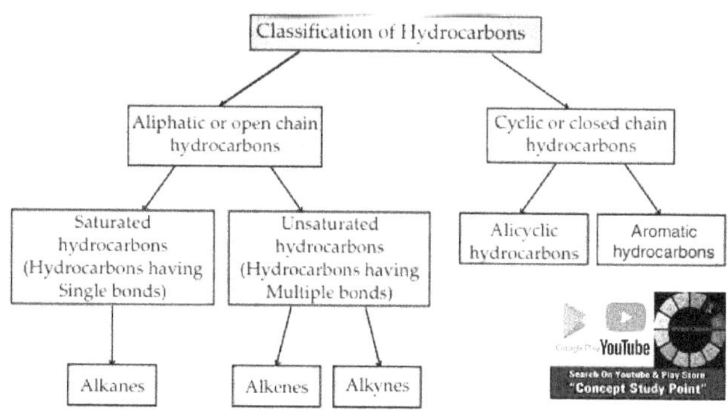

❑❑

SOME IMPORTANT QUESTIONS

Q1. C_3H_8 belongs to the homologous series of

(a) Alkynes (b) Alkenes (c) Alkanes (d) Cyclo alkanes

Q2. A hydrocarbon has four carbon atoms. Give its molecular formula if it is an alkene.

(a) C_4H_{10} (b) C_4H_8 (C) C_4H_6 (d) C_4H_4

Q3. Name the functional group present in CH_3COCH_3.

(a) Alcohol (b) Carboxylic acid (c) Ketone (d) Aldehyde

Q4. Which of the following belongs to homologous series of alkynes? C_6H_6, C_2H_6, C_2H_4, C_3H_4.

(a) C_6H_6 (b) C_2H_4 (C) C_2H_6 (d) C_3H_4

Q5. The first member of the alkyne homologous series is

(a) propyne (b) ethyne (c) methane (d) ethane

Q6. —CHO represents the functional group

(a) esters (b) carboxylic acid (c) alcohols (d) aldehydes

Q7. The name of an alcohol with three carbon atoms in its molecule is:

(i) Methanol (ii) Ethanol (iii) Propanol (iv) Butanol

Q8. Which of these will contain covalent double between its atoms?

(i) H2 (ii) O2 (iii) Cl2 (iv) Nacl

Q9. Identify the unsaturated compounds from the following:

(i) Propane (ii) Propene (iii) Propyne (iv) Chloropropane

(a) (i) and (ii) (b) (ii) and (iv) (c) (iii) and (iv) (d) (ii) and (iii)

Q10. In the soap micelles :

(a) the ionic end of soap is on the surface of the cluster while the carbon chain is in the interior of the cluster.

(b) ionic end of soap is in the interior of the cluster and the carbon chain is out of the cluster. (c) both ionic end and carbon chain are in the interior of the cluster.

(d) both ionic end and carbon chain are on the exterior of the cluster.

Q11. Pentane has the molecular formula C_5H_{12} it has:

(a) 5 Covalent Bonds (b) 12 Covalent Bonds

(c) 16 Covalent Bonds (d) 17 Covalent Bonds

Q12.

Structural formula of benzene is :

(a) 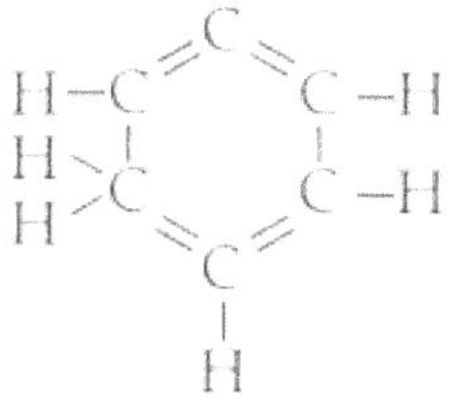
```
          C
H—C //      \\ C—H
H \ |          |
H / C          C—H
      \\     //
          C
          |
          H
```

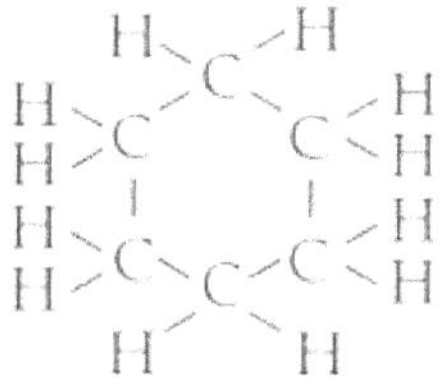

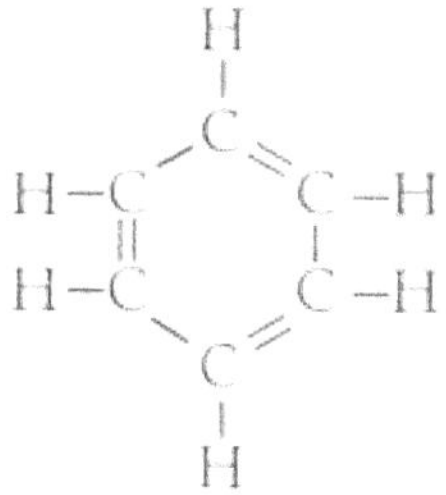

(b)
```
      H       H
        \ C /
H \  /      \  / H
H / C        C \ H
    |        |   / H
H \ C \    / C \ H
H /     C
      H    H
```

(c)
```
          H
          |
          C
H—C  /      \\ C—H
   ||          |
H—C            C—H
      \      //
          C
          |
          H
```

(d) 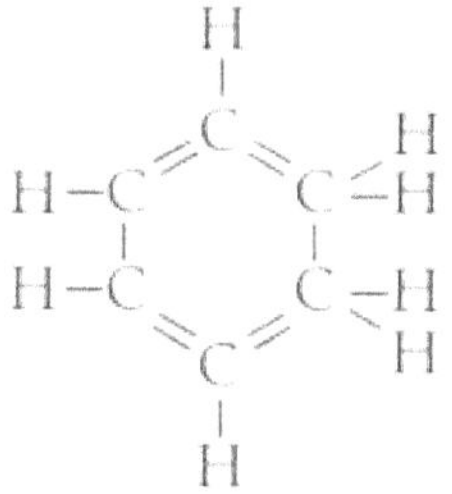
```
          H
          |
          C              H
H—C //      \\ C /—H
   |           |
H—C            C —H
     \\      //  \ H
          C
          |
          H
```

Q13. Which among the following are unsaturated hydrocarbons?

(i) $H_3C-CH_2-CH_2-CH_3$

(ii) $H_3C-C \equiv C-CH_3$

iii) $H_3C-\underset{\displaystyle CH_3}{\underset{|}{CH}}-CH_3$

iv) $H_3C-\underset{\displaystyle CH_3}{\underset{|}{C}}=CH_2$

(a) (i) and (iii)
(b) (ii) and (iii)
(c) (ii) and (iv)
(d) (iii) and (iv)

Q14.Carbon has four electrons in its valence shell. How does carbon attain stable electronic configuration? [CBSE 2015]

Q15. Draw electron dot structure of water molecule.

Q16. Which element exhibits the property of catenation to the maximum extent and why? [Foreign 2016]

Q17. Write the electron dot structure of the ethane molecule (C_2H_6). [Delhi 2011]

Q18. Name the following:

(a) A metal, which is preserved in kerosene.

(b) A lustrous coloured non-metal.

(c) A metal, which can melt while kept on the palm.

(d) A metal, which is a poor conductor of heat.

Q19. A metal 'X' acquires a green colour coating on its surface on exposure to air.

(i) Identify the metal 'X' and name the process responsible for this change.

(ii)Name and write the chemical formula of the green coating formed on the metal.

(iii) List two important methods to prevent the process.

Q20. (a) Write the chemical name of the coating that forms on silver and copper articles when these are left exposed to moist air.

(b) Explain what galvanization is. What purpose is served by it?

(c) Define an alloy. How are alloys prepared? How do the properties of iron change when:

(i) small quantity of carbon,

(ii) nickel and chromium are mixed with it.

Q21. Give reasons for the following:

(i) Silver and copper lose their shine when they are exposed to air. Name the substance formed on their surface in each case.

(ii) Tarnished copper vessels are cleaned with tamarind juice.

(iii) Aluminium is more reactive than iron yet there is less corrosion of aluminium as compared to iron when both are exposed to air.

Q22. Write two differences between calcination and roasting.

Answers

1	2	3	4	5	6	7	8	9	10	11	12	13
C	B	C	D	B	D	C	B	D	A	C	C	C

Ans 14.

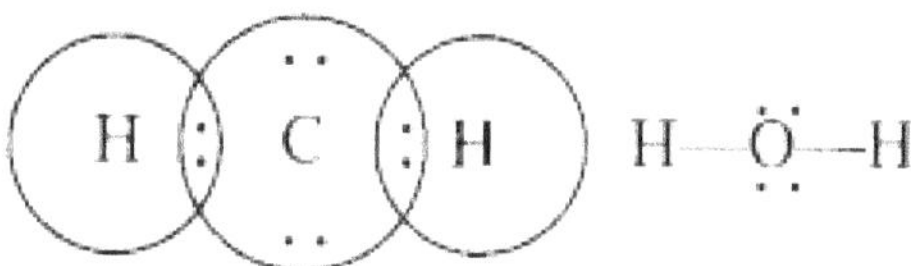

Ans 15. Carbon shows catenation to a maximum extent because it forms strong covalent bonds.

Ans 16.

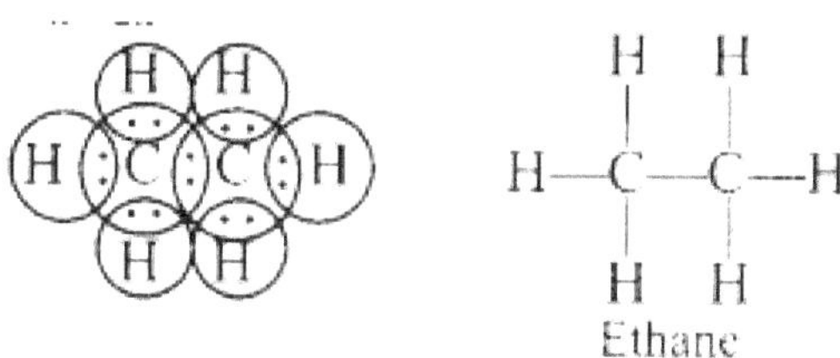

Ans 17. (a) Sodium is preserved in kerosene.

(b) Iodine is lustrous colored non-metal.

(c) Gallium.

(d) Lead.

Ans 18. (i) Metal is copper. The process is corrosion.

(ii)Basic copper carbonate [$CuCO_3.Cu(OH)_2$].

(iii)• It should be coated with tin

• It should be mixed with other metals to form alloys.

Ans 19. (a) Ag_2S (silver sulphide) is formed on silver, basic copper carbonate $CuCO_3$. $CU(OH)_2$ is formed on copper.

(b) The process of coating zinc over iron is called galvanization. It is used to prevent rusting of iron.

(c) Alloy is a homogeneous mixture of two or more metals. One of them can be non-metal. Alloys are prepared by melting two or more metals together.

(I) Iron does not rust on adding the small, quantity of carbon.

(ii) When we form an alloy of iron with nickel and chromium, we get stainless steel which is malleable and does not get rusted.

Ans 20. (i) These metals get corroded. Silver forms black Ag2S (silver sulphide) and copper forms a greenish layer of basic copper carbonate

$CuCO_3$. $CU(OH)_2$

(ii) Tamarind contains acid which reacts with basic copper carbonate and the product gets dissolved and removed from the copper vessel.

(in) Aluminium forms an oxide layer on its surface which does not further react with air.

Ans 21.

Roasting	***Calcination***
Ore is heated in excess of air.	Ore is heated in the absence or limited supply of air.
This is used for sulphide ores.	This is used for carbonate ores.
SO_2 is produced along with metal oxide.	CO_2 is produced along with metal oxide.
e.g. $2ZnS + 3O_2 \xrightarrow{\Delta} 2ZnO + 2SO_2$	e.g. $ZnCO_3 \xrightarrow{\Delta} ZnO + CO_2$

II

Periodic classification of elements

Chapter-5

1. Classification means identifying similar species and grouping them together.
2. Lavoisier divided elements into two main types known as metals and non-metals.
3. Doberiner's Law of Triads: According to this law, "in certain triads (grout) of three elements) the atomic mass of the central element was the arithmetic mean of the atomic masses of the other two elements." But in some triads all the three elements possessed nearly the same atomic masses, therefore the law was rejected.
e.g., atomic masses of Li, Na and K are respectively 7, 23 and 39, thus the mean of atomic masses of I St and 3rd element is 23.

Elements	Atomic Mass
Ca	40.1
Sr	87.6
Ba	137.3

Limitations of Doberiner's Triads

Only three traids were recognized from the elements known at that time.

(i) Li, Na, K

(ii) Ca, Sr, Ba

(iii) Cl, Br, I

4. Newland's Law of Octaves:

According to this law "the elements are arranged in such a way that the eighth element starting from a given one has properties which are a repetition of those of the first if arranged in order of increasing atomic weight like the. eight note of the musical scale."

sa (do)	re (re)	ga (mi)	ma (fa)	pa (so)	da (la)	ni (ti)
H	Li	Be	B	C	N	O
F	Na	Mg	Al	Si	P	S
Cl	K	Ca	Cr	Ti	Mn	Fe
Co and Ni	Cu	Zn	Y	In	As	Se
Br	Rb	Sr	Ce and La	Zr	—	—

Newland's Law of Octaves

The drawback of Newland's law of Octaves:

(i) According to Newland only 56 elements exist in nature and no more elements would be discovered in the future. But later on, several new elements were discovered whose properties did not fit into the law of octaves.

(ii) In order to fit new elements into his table Newland adjust two elements in the same column, but put some unlike elements under the same column.

Thus, Newland"s classification was not accepted.

Mendeleev's Periodic Table :

Mendeleev arranged 63 elements known at that time in the periodic table. According to Mendeleev "the properties of the elements are a periodic function of their atomic masses." The table consists of eight vertical columns called „groups" and horizontal rows called „periods".

Merits of Mendeleev's Periodic Table:

(i) At some places the order of atomic weight was changed in order to justify the chemical and physical nature.

(ii) Mendeleev left some gaps for new elements which were not discovered at that time.

(iii) One of the strengths of Mendeleev's periodic table was that when inert gases were discovered they could be placed in a new group without disturbing the existing order.

Characteristics of the periodic table: Its main characteristics are :

(i) In the periodic table, the elements are arranged in vertical rows called groups and horizontal rows called periods.

(ii) There are eight groups indicated by Roman Numerals I, II, III, IV, V,

VI, VII, VIII. The elements belonging to the first seven groups have been divided into sub-groups designated as A and B on the basis of similarities. The elements that are present on the left-hand side in each group constitute sub-group A while those on the right-hand side form sub-group B. Group VIII consists of nine elements arranged in three triads.

(iii) There are six periods (numbered 1, 2, 3, 4, 5, and 6). In order to accommodate more elements, periods 4, 5, 6 are divided into two halves. The first half of the elements are placed in the upper left corners and the second half occupies the lower right corners in each box.

Achievements of Mendeleev's periodic table

(i) The arrangement of elements in groups and periods made the study of elements

quite systematic in the sense that if properties of one element in a particular group are known, those of the others can be easily predicted.

(ii) Prediction of new elements and their properties: Many gaps were left in this table for undiscovered elements. However, the properties of these elements could be predicted in advance from their expected position. This helped in the discovery of these elements. The elements silicon, gallium and germanium were discovered in this manner.

(iii) Correction of doubtful atomic masses: Mendeleev corrected the atomic masses of certain elements with the help of their expected positions and properties.

Limitations of Mendeleev's classification:

(i) He could not assign a correct position of hydrogen in his periodic table, as the properties of hydrogen resemble both alkali metals as well as with halogens.

(ii) The isotopes of the same element will be given different positions if the atomic number is taken as a basis, which will disturb the symmetry of the periodic table.

(iii) The atomic masses do not increase in a regular manner in going from one element to the next. So it was not possible to predict how many elements could be discovered between two elements

6. Modern Periodic Law: This law was given by Henry Moseley in 1913. it states, "Properties of the elements are the periodic function of their atomic numbers".

Cause of periodicity: Periodicity may be defined as the repetition of the similar properties of the elements placed in a group and separated by a certain definite gap of atomic numbers.

The cause of periodicity is the resemblance in properties of the elements is the repetition of the same valence shell electronic configuration.

7. Modern Periodic Table

Moseley proposed this modern periodic table according to which "the physical and chemical properties of elements are periodic function of their atomic number and not the horizontal rows called "periods". The groups have been numbered 1, 2, 3 .... 18 from left to right.

(ii) The elements belonging to a particular group make a family and are usually named after the first member. In a group, all the elements contain the same number of valence electrons.

(iii) In a period all the elements contain the same number of shells, but as we move from left to right the number of valence shell electrons increases by one unit. The maximum number of electrons that can be accommodated in a shell can be calculated by the formula 2n2 where n is the number of the given shell from the nucleus.

8. Trends in Modern Periodic Table :

The trends observed in some important properties of the elements in moving down the group (from top to bottom of the table) and across a period (from left to right in a period) are discussed below :

(i) Valency: Valency may be defined as the combining capacity of the atom of an element with atoms of other elements in order to acquire the stable configuration (i.e. 8 electrons in the valence shell. In some special cases it is 2 electrons).

Third period elements	Na	Mg	Al	Si	P	S	Cl	Ar
Valency	1	2	3	4	3	2	1	0

(ii) Atomic size: It refers to the distance between the center of the nucleus of an isolated atom to its outermost shell containing electrons. The atomic radius decreases on moving from left to right along a period. This is due to an increase in nuclear charge which tends to pull the electrons closer to the nucleus and reduces the size of the atom. In a group, atomic size decreases from top to bottom due to an increase in the number of shells.

Third period elements	Na	Mg	Al	Si	P	S	Cl
Atomic radii (Pm)	186	160	143	118	110	104	99

(iii) Metallic and non-metallic properties: In a period from left to right metallic nature decreases while non-metallic character increases.

In a group metallic character increases from top to bottom while non-metallic character decrease.

(iv) Electronegativity: The relative tendency of an atom to attract the shared electron pair of electrons towards itself is called electronegativity.

In a period from left to right, the value of electronegativity increases while in a group from top to bottom the value of electronegativity decreases.

Property	Atomic Size	Metallic character	Non-metallic character
Variation across Periods	Decreases	Decreases	Increases
Reason	Due to increase in nuclear charge, or resulting in stronger force of attraction which causes shrinking.	Due to increase in effective nuclear charge, tendency to lose valence electrons decreases.	Due to increase in effective nuclear charge, tendency to gain electrons increases.
Variation along Groups	Increases	Increases	Decreases
Reason	Due to addition of new shells, the distance between outermost electron and nucleus increases.	Decrease in effective nuclear charge experienced by valence electrons. Tendency to lose electrons increases.	Due to decrease in effective nuclear charge experienced by valence electrons (due to addition of new shells) tendency to gain electrons decreases.

Very Important Questions

Q1. Newlands relation is called

(a) Musical Law (b) Law of Octaves (c) Periodic Law (d) Atomic Mass Law

Q2. What is the atomic number of elements of period 3 and group 17 of the Periodic Table?

(a) 10 (b) 4 (c) 17 (d) 21

Q3. Which one of the following statements is not correct about the trends in the properties of the elements of a period on going from left to right?

(a) The oxides become more acidic

(b) The elements become less metallic

(c) There is an increase in the number of valence electrons

(d) The atoms lose their electrons more easily

Q4. A metal 'M' is in the first group of the Periodic Table. What will be the formula of its oxide?

(a) MO (b) M_2O (C) $M2O_3$ (d) MO_2

Q5. Name the neutral atom in the Periodic Table which has the same number of electrons as K+ and Cl-.

(a) Helium (b) Argon (c) Neon (d) Krypton

Q6. An element X has mass number 40 and contains 21 neutrons in its atom. To which group of the Periodic Table does it belong?

(a) Group 1 (b) Group 4 (c) Group 2 (d) Group 3

Q7. According to Mendeleev's Periodic Law, the elements were arranged in the periodic table in the order of:

(a) increasing atomic number (b) decreasing atomic number

(c) increasing atomic masses (d) decreasing atomic masses

Q8. Modern Periodic law is based upon:

(a) Number of neutrons (b) Number of electron

(c) Atomic number (d) Atomic mass

Q9. Which of the following set of elements is written in order of their increasing metallic character?

(a) Na Li K (b) C Q N (c) Mg Al Si (d) Be Mg Ca

Q10. The non-metals are present:

(a) On the right-hand side of the periodic table.

(b) In the middle of the periodic table.

(c) In the center of the periodic table.

(d) On the left-hand side of the periodic table.

Q11. An element has 12 protons. The group and period to which this element belongs to is

(a) 2nd group, 3rd period (b) 2nd group, 2nd period
(c) 3rd group, 2nd period (d) 3rd group, 3rd period

Q12. Which of the following is the outermost shell for elements of the second period?
(a) K shell (b) L shell (c) M shell (d) N shell

Q13. Pick out the chemically most reactive elements from the given triads.
Li, Na, K F, Cl, Br
(a) Li and F (b) Li and Br (c) K and F (d) K and Br

Q14. n atom of an element has the electronic configuration 2,8,2. To which group does it belong?
(a) 4th group (b) 6th group (c) 3rd group (d) 2nd group

Q15. New lands relation is called
(a) Musical Law (b) Law of Octaves
(c) Periodic Law (d) Atomic Mass Law

Q16. Which has a larger atomic radius Ca (20) or K (19). [CBSE 2016]

Q17. An element has atomic number 17 to which group and the period closer it belongs. [CBSE 2016]

Q18. H, Li. Na, K placed in a group. Why? [CBSE 2015]

Q19. Fill in the blanks

1. The concept of grouping elements into triads was given by ....
2. Mendeleev's basis for the Periodic Table is ....
3. The basis for Modern Periodic Table is ....
4. (a) Metallic character .... down the group.
(b) Atomic size .... along the period.
(c) Electronegative character .... down the group.
5. Isotopes belong to the same .... in the Periodic Table.
6. Halogens belong to group .... of the Periodic Table.

Q20. The elements of the second period of the Periodic Table are given below:
Li Be B C N O F
(a) Give a reason to explain why atomic radii decrease from Li to F.
(b) Identify the most
(i) metallic and
(ii)non-metallic element

Q21. The position of three elements A, B, and C in the Periodic Table is shown below:
Giving reasons, explain the following:

(a) Element A is non-metal.
(b) Element B has a larger atomic size than element C.
(c) Element C has a valency of 1

Group 16	Group 17
–	–
–	A
–	–
B	C

Q22. (a) Why do we classify elements?
(b) What were the two criteria used by Mendeleev in creating his Periodic Table?
(c) Why did Mendeleev leave some gaps in his Periodic Table?
(d) In Mendeleev's Periodic Table, why was there no mention of Noble gases like Helium, Neon, and Argon?
(e) Would you place the two isotopes ' of chlorine, CI-35, and CI-37 in different slots because of their different atomic masses or in the same slot because their chemical properties are the same? Justify your answer.

Q23. Chlorine, bromine, and iodine form a Dobereiner's triad. The atomic masses of chlorine and iodine are 35.5 and 126.9 respectively. Predict the atomic mass of bromine.

ANSWERS

1	2	3	4	5	6	7	8	9	10	11	12	13	14	15
B	C	D	B	B	A	C	C	D	A	A	B	C	D	B

Ans 16. K (19) has a larger atomic radius due to a less effective number
...oe.

Ans 17. Its electronic configuration is 2, 8, 7. It belongs to group 17 because it has 7 valence electrons. It belongs to 3rd period because it has 3 shells.

Ans 18. It is because they have the same number of valence electrons i.e. 1

Ans 19.

1. Dobereiner
2. Atomic mass
3. Atomic no.
4. (a) Increases
(b) decreases
(c) decreases
5. Position
6. 17

Ans 20. a) It is because nuclear charge increases due to an increase in atomic number, therefore, the force of attraction between nucleus and valence electrons increases, i.e. effective nuclear charge increases, hence atomic radii decrease from Li to F.

(b) (i) most metallic element is 'Li' as it can lose electrons easily due to its larger atomic size.

(ii) most non-metallic element is 'F' because it can gain electrons easily due to the smallest atomic size.

Ans 21. (a) 'A' is non-metal because it can gain electrons easily as it has 7 valence electrons and forms a negative ion with a stable electronic configuration.

(b) It is because 'B' has a lesser atomic number, less nuclear charge, less force of attraction between valence electrons and nucleus, therefore, has larger atomic size.

(c) 'C' has 7 valence electrons. It can gain one electron to become stable. So, its valency is equal to one.

Ans 22. (a) It is done so as to study the properties of elements conveniently.

(b) Increasing order of atomic mass and similarities in chemical properties (especially nature and formulae of oxide and hydride formed).

(c) These gaps were left for undiscovered elements.

(d) Noble gases were not invented at that time.

(e) They will be kept at the same slot as they have same chemical properties.

Ans 23. Atomic mass of Br = (35.5+126.9)/2

= 162.4/2

= 81.2

ꕤ

III

How do organisms reproduce?

Chapter-8

Reproduction

Reproduction is an integral feature of all living beings. The process by which a living being produces its own like is called reproduction.

Importance of Reproduction:

Reproduction is important for each species, because this is the only way for a living being to continue its lineage. Apart from being important for a particular individual, reproduction is also important for the whole ecosystem. Reproduction helps in maintaining a proper balance among various biotic constituents of the ecosystem. Moreover, reproduction also facilitates evolution because variations come through reproduction; over several generations.

Types of Reproduction:

There are two main types, viz. asexual and sexual reproduction.

Asexual Reproduction: When a single parent is involved and no gamete formation takes place; the method is called asexual reproduction. No meiosis happens during asexual reproduction.

Sexual Reproduction: When two parents are involved and gamete formation takes; the method is called sexual reproduction. Meiosis happens during gamete formation; which is an important step of sexual reproduction.

Reproduction in Simple Organisms

Binary Fission: Most unicellular animals prefer this method for reproduction. These organisms reproduce by binary fission; especially when conditions are favorable, i.e. adequate amount of food and moisture is available. Binary fission is somewhat similar to mitosis. The mother cell divides into two daughter cells, and each daughter cell begins its life as a new individual. The parent generation ceases to exist, after binary fission. Amoeba is a very good example of an organism that reproduces by binary fission.

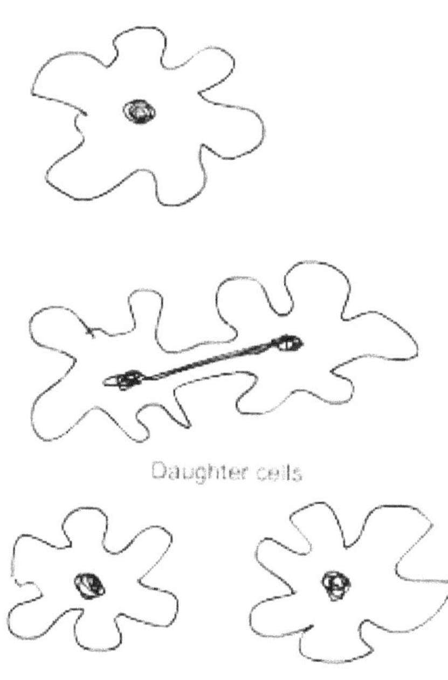

Binary Fission in Ameoba

Multiple Fission: When conditions become unfavorable, i.e. food, moisture, proper temperature, etc. are not available; this is the preferred mode of reproduction by unicellular organisms. The organism develops a thick coating around itself. This is called cyst. The cyst helps the organism to tide over the bad phase. The nucleus divides into several nuclei and each daughter nucleus is surrounded by a membrane. All metabolic activities stop in the organism, after cyst formation. When favorable conditions return, the cyst dissolves or breaks down; releasing the daughter nuclei. The daughter nuclei; in turn; grow into new individuals. Plasmodium and entamoeba undergo cyst stage, when they are not in the body of their prime host, i.e. humans.

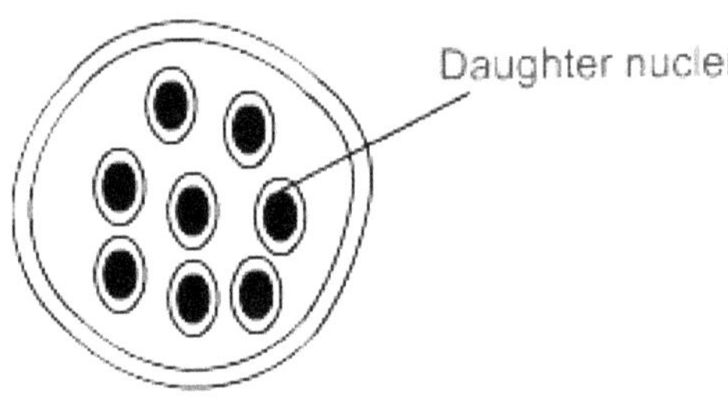

Multiple fission

Budding: Yeast is an example of a unicellular organism that reproduces by budding. Hydra is an example of a multicellular organism that reproduces by this method.

Budding in Yeast: A small bud grows at any end of the yeast cell. Nucleus gets elongated and a part of it protrudes into the bud. The nucleus then divides into two nuclei. One of the nuclei goes into the bud. The bud grows to a certain extent and gets detached from the mother cell.

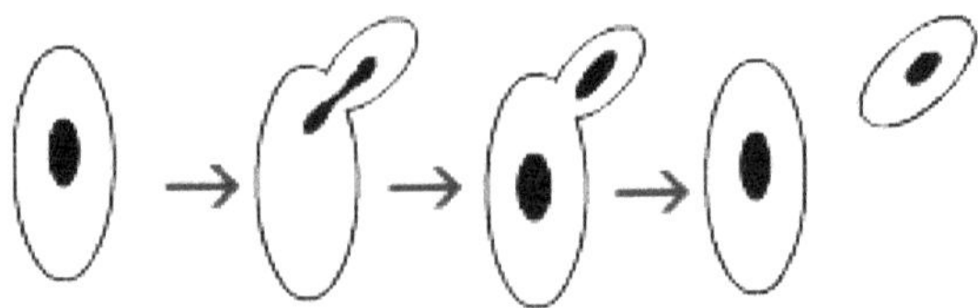

Budding in Yeast

Budding in Hydra: A bud grows anywhere on the main body of the hydra. The bud grows to a certain size and gets detached from the mother hydra. This develops further to grow into a new individual.

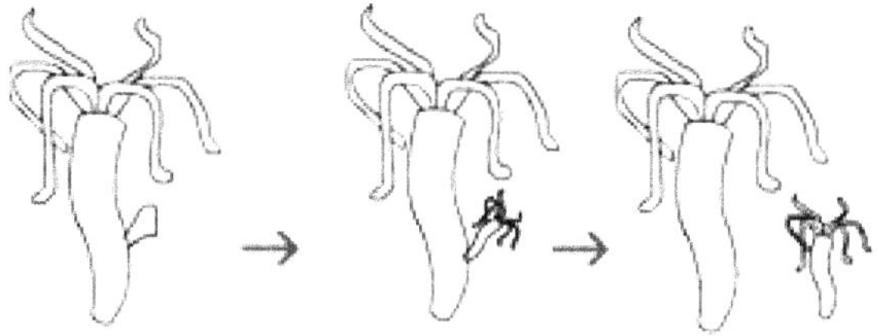

Budding in Hydra

Fragmentation: Reproduction by fragmentation is seen in filamentous algae, e.g. spirogyra. The filament of spirogyra divides into many pieces and each piece develops into a new individual.

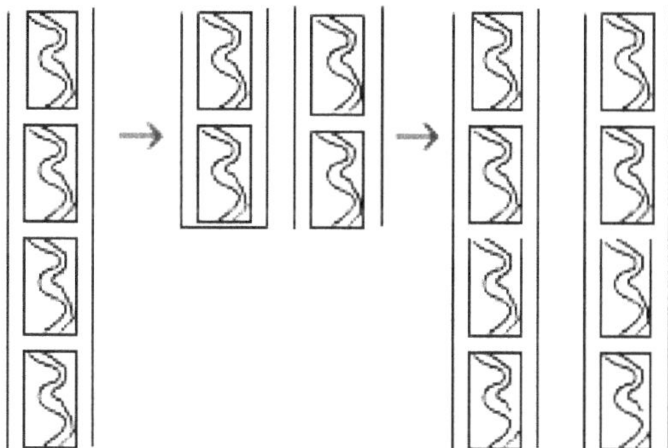

Fragmentation

Spore Formation: Most of the fungi, bryophytes, and pteridophytes reproduce by this method. Spores are produced in special spore-bearing organs; called sporangium. When spores mature; the sporangium bursts open to release them.

Advantages of Spore Formation: In fact, spores give certain survival benefits to the organisms which reproduce by spores. Spores can be disseminated through air and water or even through some other carriers; like animals. This helps an organism to spread its presence to a wider geographical area. Spores can also remain dormant for a long time, till favorable conditions are found. Scientists consider spores are precursors of seeds.

Vegetative Propagation: Vegetative propagation is a special case, as it happens in higher plants; which otherwise have the capability to reproduce sexually. When a vegetative part of a flowering plant reproduces a new plant, it is called vegetative propagation. Some examples of vegetative propagation are given below.

A tuber of Potato: The potato tuber is a modified stem. Many notches can be seen on the surface of potatoes. These are called 'eyes' of potatoes. Each 'eye' of a potato can give rise to a new potato plant. Farmers utilize this capability of potatoes to grow potatoes more quickly; which is not possible by using the seeds of potato.

Modified roots of Carrot and Sweet Potato: Carrot and sweet potato are examples of modifications of roots; for food storage. These roots can give rise to new plants; when kept under the soil.

Rhizomes of Ginger and Turmeric: Rhizomes are examples of modified underground stems for food storage. These contain nodes, internodes, and scaly leaves. When buried under the soil, the rhizomes produce new plants.

Leaf of Bryophyllum: Leaves of bryophyllum have notches on the margin. If a leaf is put under the soil, small saplings grow from the notches on the leaf margin.

Artificial Vegetative Propagation: Man has used artificial vegetative propagation to grow many plants. This has enabled farmers and horticulturists to grow many plants in a shorter duration and has helped them to earn more profit. Artificial vegetative propagation has also helped in developing many new varieties of plants. Stem cutting, layering, and grafting are the preferred means of artificial vegetative propagation.

Advantages of Asexual Reproduction:

- The organism does not have to depend on another organism for carrying out reproduction; because a single parent is needed.
- It takes less time than sexual reproduction and hence more offspring can be produced in a shorter time.
- The offspring are exact clones of their parent.
- Desirable characteristics can be easily incorporated into plants with artificial vegetative propagation.

Disadvantages of Asexual Reproduction:

- As a single parent is involved, there is a negligible chance of variation.
- In most cases in simple organisms, the parent generation ceases to exist after asexual reproduction.
- Asexual reproduction cannot give rise to biodiversity which is important for a healthy ecosystem.

Sexual Reproduction and Variations:

As discussed earlier, sexual reproduction involves two parents and gamete formation. Gametes are special cells that are formed after meiosis. There are two types of gametes, viz. male and female gametes. The number of chromosomes is haploid in the gametes. When gametes fuse during fertilization, the number of chromosomes becomes diploid. This is important for maintaining the unique identity of a particular species which reproduces by the sexual method.

In sexual reproduction, the offspring gets sets of genes from two different individuals. This leads to subtle variation through subsequent generations. These variations accumulate over thousands of generations and finally may give rise to a new species. That is how all complex organisms have evolved from a common ancestor.

DNA Replication:

DNA replication is the process by which DNA makes a copy of itself. DNA replication happens during the S – phase (synthesis phase) of the cell cycle. This is important because the daughter cells would need additional copies of the DNA. The process of DNA replication is a foolproof process, yet some alterations do take place. These alterations may lead to some variations in the characters of the daughter cells.

Sexual Reproduction in Flowering Plants:

The flower is a modified leaf that bears special organs and plays the role of the reproductive system in the plant.

Structure of a typical Flower:

A typical flower is composed of four distinct whorls, viz. calyx, corolla, androecium, and gynoecium.

Calyx: The outermost whorl of the flower is called the calyx. It is composed of green leaf-like structures; called sepals.

Corolla: The second whorl of the flower is called the corolla. It is composed of colourful leaf-like structures; called petals. Petals are colourful so that insects and birds can be attracted; to assist the flower in pollination.

Androecium: This is the third whorl in the flower. It is composed of stamens. Stamen is made of a slender stalk and anthers on top. Anthers produce pollen grains. Pollen grains are the male gametes.

Gynoecium: This whorl is at the center of the flower. It is composed of a swollen base; called the ovary. A slender style stands upright on the ovary. It has a flat top; called stigma. Ovules are inside the ovary. Ovules are the female gametes.

Pollination: The pollen grains need to be transferred to the stigma so that fertilization can take place. The transfer of pollen grains from anther to the stigma is called pollination. If the pollen grains from the same flower or the same plant are transferred to the stigma; it is called self-pollination. If pollen grains from a different plant are transferred to the stigma; it is called cross-pollination. Cross-pollination is better; from the perspective of variations. Many agents help plants in cross-pollination, e.g. insects, animals, air, water, etc. Insects are the main pollinators for the plant kingdom.

Fertilization:

The fusion of male and female gametes is called fertilization. The product of fertilization is called zygote. A zygote undergoes several rounds of mitosis and develops into an embryo. Subsequently, the embryo develops into a new individual.

Fertilization in flowering plants:

After landing at the stigma, pollen grains absorb moisture and germinate. A pollen grain develops a pollen tube; which penetrates through the tissue of the style and reaches the ovule. Pollen nuclei are transferred through the pollen tube. After fertilization, the zygote is formed; which finally develops into the embryo.

Changes in flower; After Fertilization: The calyx and corolla wither and fall off and so do the stamens. The ovary turns into the fruit. The embryo turns into a seed. Once the seed becomes mature, fruit dries up so that dispersal of seeds can take place.

Structure of Seed: A seed contains an embryo, some reserved food, and is enclosed by a protective covering; called a seed coat. The reserve food is stored in the cotyledons. The embryo has two pointed parts. The upper part is called plumule which gives rise to the shoot system. The lower part is called the radicle which gives rise to the root system. Cotyledons supply food when the embryo needs it during germination. Seed germination is the process by which the embryo in the seed kick-starts a new life.

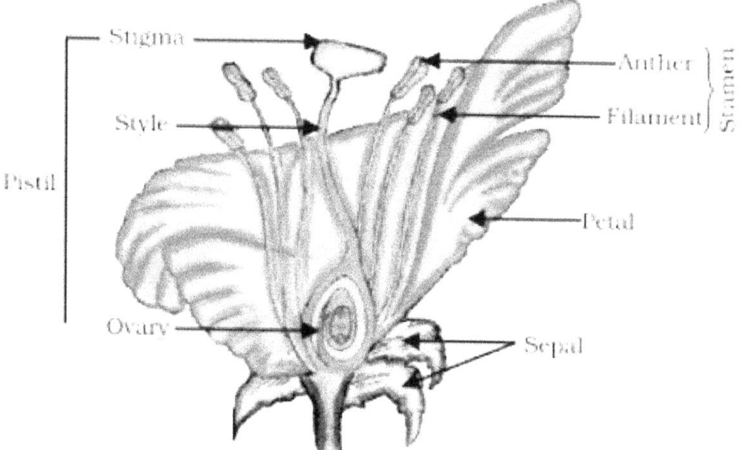

Longitudinal section of lower

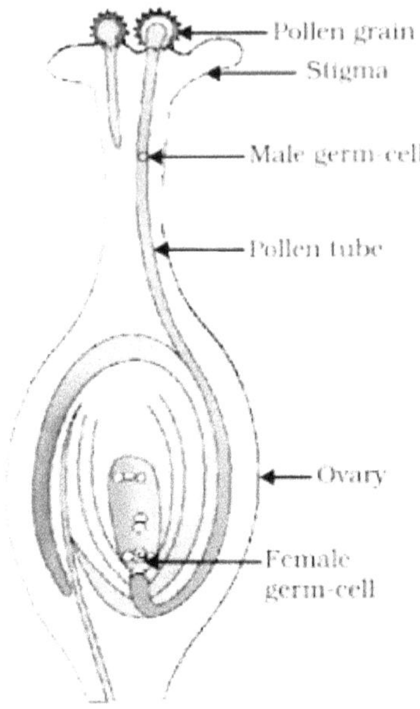

Germination of pollen on stigma

Reproduction in Human Beings

Humans use a sexual mode of reproduction.

Sexual maturation: The period of life when the production of germ cells i.e. ova (female) and sperm (male) starts in the body. This period of sexual maturation is called puberty.

Changes at Puberty:

- Common in male and female

→ Thick hair growth in armpits and genital area.

→ Skin becomes oily, may result in pimples.

- In girls

→ Breast size begins to increase.

→ Girls begin to menstruate.

- In boys

→ Thick hair growth on face.

→ Voice begins to crack.

These changes signal that sexual maturity is taking place.

Male Reproductive System:

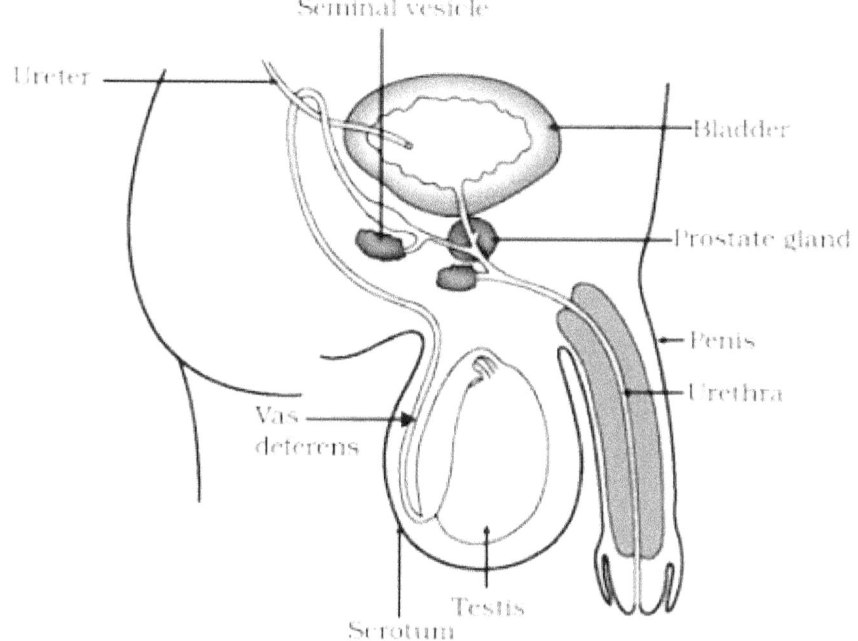

Human–male reproductive system

The male reproductive system in human beings is composed of the following parts:

Testis: There is a pair of testes; which lie in a skin pouch; called the scrotum. The scrotum is suspended outside the body; below the abdominal cavity. This helps in maintaining the temperature of testes below the body temperature. This is necessary for optimum sperm production. Testis primarily serves the function of sperm production. Sperms are the male gametes. Apart from that, testis also produces testosterone. Testosterone is also called the male hormone, as it is responsible for developing certain secondary sexual characters in boys.

Vas Deferens: Vas deferens is the tube that carries sperms to the seminal vesicle.

Seminal Vesicle: This is the place where sperms are stored. Secretions from the seminal vesicle and prostate gland add up to make the semen.

Penis: It is a muscular organ that serves the genitor-urinary functions. The urethra works as the common passage for urine as well as for sperms.

Female Reproductive System:

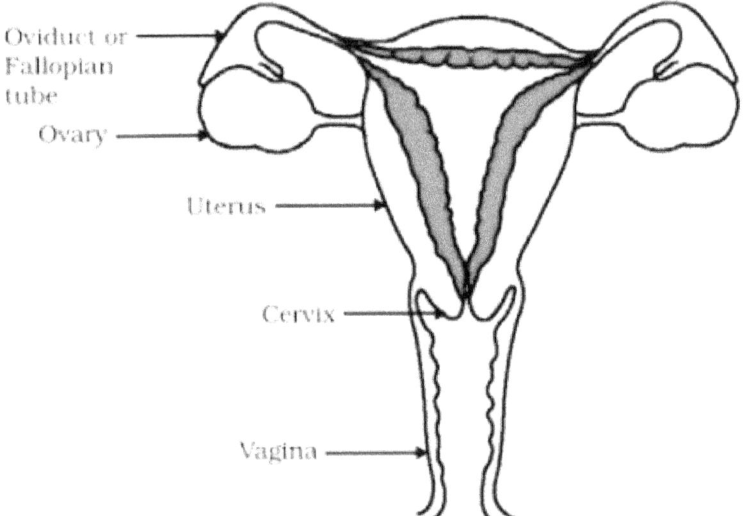

Human–female reproductive system

The female reproductive system in human beings is composed of the following parts:

Uterus: This is a pear-shaped hollow muscular organ. The uterus is the place where the embryo gets implanted and develops into a newborn baby. The wall of the uterus provides safety and nutrition to the growing foetus.

Fallopian Tubes: One fallopian tube comes out from each side at the top of the uterus. The fallopian tubes end in finger-like structures; called fimbriae. Fertilization happens in the fallopian tube.

Ovary: There are two ovaries; one near each fallopian tube. The ovary produces the eggs or the female gametes. All the eggs are produced by the ovary when the female child is still in the womb. One egg matures in each ovulation cycle and is released from the ovary. The egg is caught by the fimbriae and transferred to the fallopian tube.

Vagina: The cervix (mouth of the uterus) opens into the vagina. The vagina is a muscular tube-like organ; which serves as the passage for the sperms and also as the canal during childbirth.

Fertilization of egg

- **When the egg is fertilized**

The fertilized egg called a zygote is planted in the uterus and develops into an embryo. The embryo gets nutrition from the mother's blood with the help of a special tissue called the placenta. It provides a large surface area for the exchange of glucose, oxygen, and waste material. The time period from fertilization up to the birth of the baby is called the gestation period. It is for about months.

- **When the egg is not fertilized**

The uterus prepares itself every month to receive a fertilized egg. The lining of the uterus becomes thick and spongy, required to support the embryo. When fertilization had not taken place, this lining is not needed any longer. This lining breaks and comes out through the vagina as blood and mucus.

Reproductive Health

Reproductive health means total well-being in all aspects of reproduction i.e. physical, emotional, social, and behavioral.

Sexually Transmitted Diseases (STDs)

Many diseases can be sexually transmitted such as:
(i) Bacterial: Gonorrhoea and syphilis
(ii) Viral: Warts and HIV-AIDS
The use of condoms prevents these infections to some extent.
Contraception: It is the avoidance of pregnancy, that can be achieved by preventing the fertilization of ova.

Methods of contraception

(i) **Physical barrier:** To prevent the union of egg and sperm. Use of condoms, cervical caps, and diaphragm.
(ii) **Chemical methods:** Use of oral pills. These change the hormonal balance of the body so that eggs are not released. May have side effects.
(iii) **Intrauterine contraceptive device (IUCD)**
Copper-T or loop is placed in the uterus to prevent pregnancy.
(iv) **Surgical methods**
→ In males, the vas deferens are blocked to prevent sperm transfer called vasectomy.

→ In females, the fallopian tube is blocked to prevent egg transfer called tubectomy

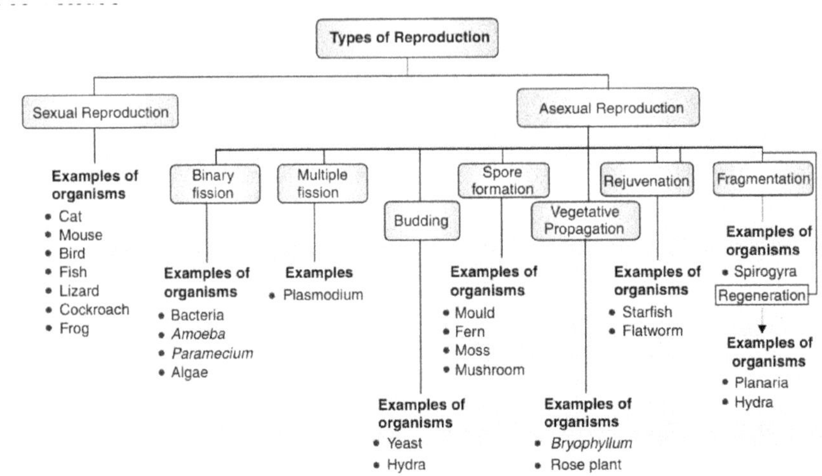

Flow Chart With Examples

SOME IMPORTANT QUESTIONS

Q1. During favourable conditions, Amoeba reproduces by
(a) multiple fission (b) binary fission (c) budding (d) fragmentation

Q2. The ability of a cell to divide into several cells during reproduction in Plasmodium is called
(a) budding (b) multiple fission (c) binary fission (d) reduction division

Q3. Bryophyllum can be propagated vegetatively by the
(a) stem (b) leaf (c) root (d) flower

Q4. Spirogyra reproduce by
(a) budding (b) fragmentation (c) regeneration (d) fission

Q5. The flower of the Hibiscus plant is
(a) bisexual (b) unisexual (c) neuter (d) very small

Q6. The process of release of eggs from the ovary is called
(a) menstruation (b) reproduction (c) insemination (d) ovulation

Q7. In human beings, fertilization occurs in the
(a) uterus (b) ovaries (c) fallopian tubes (d) vagina

Q8. A pair of ducts arising from testis, which carries sperms are
(a) fallopian tube (b) vas deferens (c) oviduct (d) urethra

Q9. When sperm is deposited into the vagina which route does it travel?
(a) Vagina → Oviduct → Uterus → Cervix (b) Vagina → Ovary → Uterus → Oviduct
(c) Vagina → Cervix → Uterus → Oviduct (d) Vagina → Uterus → Cervix → Oviduct

Q10. Which of this is seminal fluid?
(a) Prostate gland (b) Cowper's gland (c) Seminal vesicle (d) all of these

Q11. The period during adolescence when the reproductive tissues begin to mature is called
(a) ovyfetion (b) puberty (c) germination (d) propagation

Q12. In a woman, fertilization of the ovum takes place in
(a) Vagina (b) ovary (c) uterus (d) Fallopian tubes

Q13. Spirogyra reproduce by
(a) budding (b) fragmentation (c) regeneration (d) fission

Q14. During favourable conditions, Amoeba reproduces by
(a) multiple fission (b) binary fission
(c) budding (d) fragmentations

Q15. During favorable conditions, Amoeba reproduces by
(a) multiple fission (b) binary fission
(c) budding (d) fragmentations

Q16. Fill in the Blanks

1. The process of reproduction involving only one cell or one parent is called ....
2. .... is a duct coming from the urinary bladder which carries sperms.
3. Process of fertilization takes place in the .... tube in humans.
4. .... is the ability of an organism to replace its lost body parts.
5. .... is called the production of new plants from stems, roots or leaves.
6. .... is the term used to refer to the commencement of menstruation at puberty.
7. .... is the virus that causes AIDS.

Q17. What is the role of seminal vesicles and the prostate gland? [AI 2011]

Q18. Which one of the STDs damages the immune system of human body?

Q19. (i) What is fertilization? Distinguish between external fertilization and internal fertilization.
(ii) What is the site of fertilization in human beings?

Q20. "Variations that confer an advantage to an individual organism only will survive in a population." Justify.

Q21. Differentiate between 'self-pollination' and 'cross-pollination'. Describe double fertilization in plants.

Q22. a) Name the parts labeled A, B, C, D, and E.

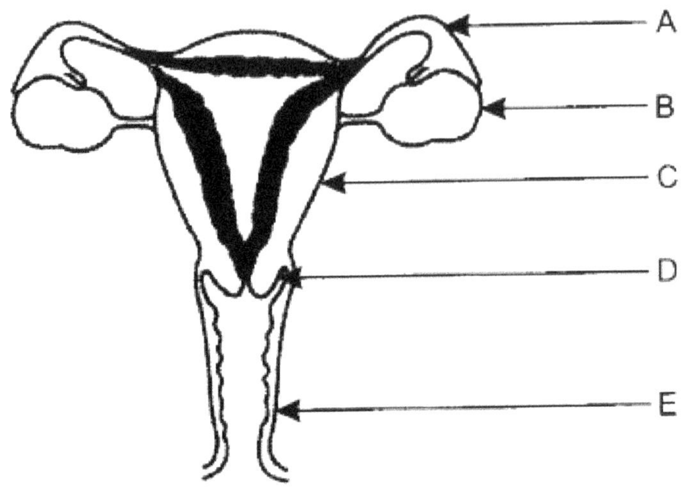

(b) Where do the following functions occur?

(i) Production of an egg

(ii) Fertilization

(iii) Implantation of zygote.

(c) What happens to the lining of the uterus:

(i) before the release of a fertilized egg?

(ii) if no fertilization occurs?

Q23. List any three differences between pollination and fertilization.

Answers:

1	2	3	4	5	6	7	8	9	10	11	12	13	14	15
B	B	B	B	A	D	C	B	C	C	B	D	B	B	A

Ans 16. 1. Uniparental/ Asexual reproduction

2. Vas deferens

3. fallopian

4. Regeneration
5. Vegetative propagation
6. Menarche
7. HIV-Human Immuno Virus

Ans 17. (i) Seminal vesicles are a pair of the thin-walled muscular elongated sacs which secrete fluid for nourishment and smooth transport of sperms.

(ii) Prostate gland also produces fluid that is released in the urethra along with the secretion of seminal vesicles to make transportation of sperms easier and also provides nutrition.

Ans 18. AIDS damages the immune system of the human body.

Ans 19. (i) Fertilization is defined as the fusion of a male gamete (sperm) with a female gamete (an ovum or egg) to form a zygote during sexual reproduction.

External Fertilisation	Internal Fertilisation
(*i*) The fusion of male gamete (sperm) and female gamete (ovum) occurs outside the body.	(*i*) The fusion of gametes occurs inside the body.
(*ii*) Both individuals discharge their gametes outside the body.	(*ii*) Only the male discharges sperms into female genital tract.
(*iii*) Development occurs outside the body.	(*iii*) Development occurs inside the body.
(*iv*) **Example:** Frog.	(*iv*) **Examples:** Human, Birds, Cattle, etc.

(ii) The site of fertilization in human beings is in the fallopian tube of the female reproductive system.

Ans 20. It is because the chances of survival depend on the nature of variations and different individuals have different kinds of advantages.
For example, bacteria that can withstand heat will survive better in a heatwave, i.e. the organisms that are fit in the competitive environment and with great variations will be able to survive and adapt. Thus, more offspring's and populations with genetic variations will survive.

Ans 21.

Self-pollination	Cross pollination
(i) Self-pollination occurs within a flower or between two flowers of the same plants.	(i) Cross-pollination occurs between two flowers borne on different plants of the same species.
(ii) Flowers do not depend on other agencies for pollination.	(ii) Agents such as insects, water and wind are required for pollination.
(iii) Pollen grains are produced in small numbers.	(iii) Pollen grains are produced in large numbers.
(iv) No wastage of pollen grains occur and thus, economical.	(iv) Wastage of pollen grains occurs and hence, not economical.
(v) Flowers are not attractive nor do they produce nectar.	(v) Flowers attract insects by various means like coloured petals, scent and nectar.
(vi) The offsprings produced are of the same genetic make up, so purity of the race is maintained.	(vi) The offsprings produced may show variations and differ in genetic make up.

During fertilization in plants, the following events take place:

(i) One of the male gametes fuses with the female gamete present in the embryo sac.

(ii) The other male gamete fuses with the two polar nuclei in the embryo sac.

The first fusion product gives rise to the zygote while the second one forms the endosperm.

The process of two fusions occurring in the embryo sac is called double fertilization.

Ans 22. (a)

A – Oviduct or Fallopian tube; B – Ovary; C – Uterus; D – Cervix; E – Vagina.

(b) (i) Ovaries; (ii) Fallopian tube;

(iii) Lining of the uterus.

(c) (i) The lining of the uterus becomes

(ii) The lining of the uterus slowly breaks and comes out through the vagina as blood and mucous, if no fertilization occurs.

Ans 23.

Pollination	Fertilisation
(*i*) It is the transfer of pollen grains from anther to the stigma of a flower.	(*i*) It is the fusion of male and female gametes.
(*ii*) Pollination precedes fertilisation.	(*ii*) Fertilisation occurs only after pollination when the pollen grains has germinated and sent the male gametes to ovule.
(*iii*) Pollination carries the male gamete producing pollen grains to the female sex organ.	(*iii*) Fertilisation brings about fusion of gametes.

IV

Heredity and Evolution

Chapter - 9

Heredity: The passing of traits from parents to offspring is called heredity. It is the heredity that is responsible for many commonly observable facts; like siblings looking similar in overall appearance.

Genotype: The complete set of genes in an organism's genome is called genotype.

Phenotype: The observable characters in an organism make the phenotype. Phenotype is a result of the genotype's interaction with the environment. Due to this reason, many phenotypes are not inheritable.

Acquired Traits: Traits; which are acquired due to interaction with the environment; are called acquired traits. Acquired traits are not inheritable. For example; if a boxer develops bulging biceps, it does not mean that his son would be borne with bulging biceps.

Inheritable Traits: Traits; which can be expressed in subsequent generations; are called inheritable traits. Such traits bring a change in the genotype of the organism and hence become inheritable.

Types of Variations

Variation is of two types:

(i) Somatic Variation

(ii) Gametic Variation

Somatic Variation:

It takes place in the body cell.

1. It is neither inherited nor transmitted.

2. It is also known as acquired traits.
3. Examples: cutting of tails in dogs, boring of pinna, etc

Gametic Variation :

1. Takes place in the gametes/Reproductive cells.
2. Inherited as well as transmitted.
3. Also known as inherited traits.
4. Example: human height, skin colour.

Accumulation of Variations during Reproduction:

Asexual reproduction involves a single parent and is hence not ideal for facilitating variations. Some minor variations do occur due to inaccuracies in DNA replication. But the quantum of variations would be too little and would take too many years to show effect.

Sexual reproduction, on the other hand, is ideal for facilitating variations because two parents are involved in it. The offspring's genotype is contributed by two parents and hence chances of variations are very high.

Rules of Inheritance

Gregor Johann Mendel conducted experiments on pea plants and proposed the rules of inheritance; based on his observations. Mendel observed that characters are often present in pairs. A pair of contrasting characters is called alleles.

Possible Reasons for Pea Plants Used by Mendel:

- Pea can be termed as a biennial plant, i.e. two generations of a pea plant can grow in a given year. This means that Mendel could get enough time to observe a larger number of generations.
- Many easily identifiable and contrasting characters are present in pea plants.
- Cross-pollination can be easily induced in pea plants.

Monohybrid Cross: The cross in which just two contrasting characters are studied is called the monohybrid cross. Mendel did a monohybrid cross for his first experiment. He selected a pair of contrasting characters for that experiment.

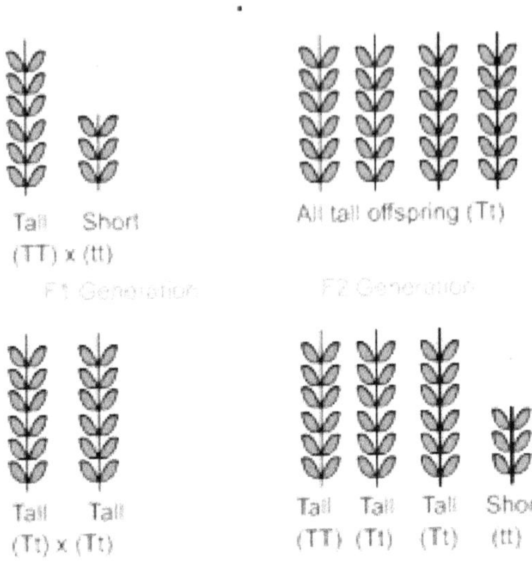

let us take the example of a cross between tall plants and short plants. The figure; given here shows the results of this experiment.

TT represents the genotype of tall plants and tt represents the genotype of short plants. In the F2 generation, all plants were tall but their genotype was Tt; which means they were not pure tall plants. This could be established by the appearance of the character of shortness in the F2 generation; in which most of the plants were tall and some of the plants were short. This experiment showed that the character of shortness of recessive in F1 generation and hence could not be observed. The ratio of the number of tall plants to that of short plants in F2 generation was 3 : 1.

Importance of Variation

Depending upon the nature of variations different individuals would have different kinds
of advantage.

For example, Bacteria that can withstand heat will survive better in a heatwave.

→ The main advantage of variation to species is that it increases the chances of its survival in a
changing environment.

→ Free ear lobes and attached ear lobes are two variants found in human populations

Mendel's First Law

Law of Segregation: Every individual possesses a pair of alleles for a particular trait. During gamete formation, a gamete receives only one trait from the alleles. A particular trait can be dominant or recessive in a particular generation.

Dihybrid Cross: The cross in which two pairs of characters are studied is called a dihybrid cross. In his second experiment, Mendel used a dihybrid cross.

Let us take an example between plants with round and green seeds and those with wrinkled and yellow seeds. **The genotype of round and green seeds is shown by RRyy and that of wrinkled and yellow seeds is shown by rrYY.** In the F1 generation, all plants produced round and yellow seeds; which means that wrinkled texture was the recessive character and so was the green colour of seeds. When plants of F1 generation were allowed to self-pollinate; it was observed that most of the plants in F2 generation produced round and yellow seeds. Some plants produce round green seeds, some produced wrinkled yellow seeds and some produced wrinkled green seeds. The ratio was 9 : 3 : 3: 1; as shown in the figure.

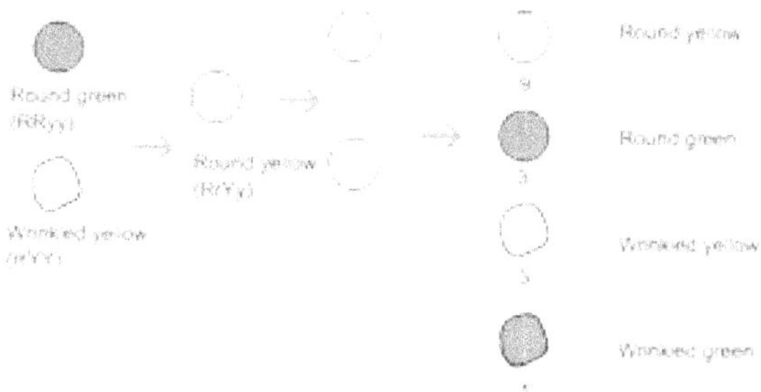

	RY	Ry	rY	ry
RY	RRYY	RRYy	RryY	RrYy
Ry	RRYy	RRyy	RrYy	Rryy
rY	RrYY	RrYy	rrYY	rrYy
ry	RrYy	Rryy	rrYy	rryy

Mendel's Second Law:

Law of Independent Assortment: Alleles of different characters separate independently from each other during gamete formation.

In the above example; alleles of texture were assorted independently from those of seed colour.

Sex Determination in Humans:

Somatic cells in human beings contain 23 pairs of chromosomes. Out of them the 23rd pair is composed of different types of chromosomes which are named as X and Y chromosomes. The 23rd pair contains one X and one Y chromosome in a male. On the other hand, the 23rd pair in a female contains X chromosomes. This means that all the eggs would have X chromosome as the 23rd chromosome, while a sperm may have either X or Y chromosome as the 23rd chromosome. When a sperm with X chromosome fertilizes the egg, the resulting zygote would develop into a female *child. When a sperm with Y chromosome fertilizes the egg, the resulting zygote would develop into a male child.*

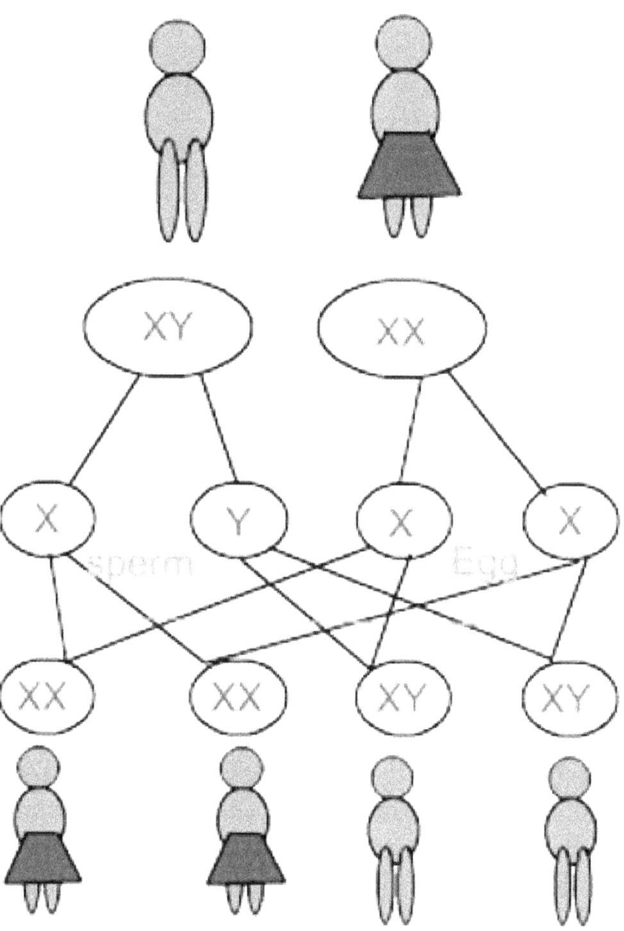

This shows that half the children will be boys and half will be girls. All children will inherit an X chromosome from their mother regardless whether they are boys or girls.

→ Thus, sex of children will be determined by what they inherit from their father, and not from their mother.

Acquired and Inherited Traits

Acquired Traits	Inherited Traits
These are the traits which are developed in an individual due to special conditions.	These are the traits which are passed from one generation to the next.
They cannot be transferred to the progeny.	They get transferred to the progeny.
They cannot direct evolution. Example: Low weight of starving beetles.	They are helpful in evolution. Example: Colour of eyes and hair.

Ways by which Speciation takes place

Speciation takes place when variation is combined with geographical isolation.

(i) **Gene flow**: Occurs between populations that are partly but not completely separated.

(ii) **Genetic drift**: It is the random change in the frequency of alleles (gene pair) in a population over successive generations.

Genetic drift takes place due to:

→ Severe changes in the DNA

→ Change in number of chromosomes

(iii) Natural selection: The process by which nature selects and consolidate those organisms which are more suitable adapted and possesses favourable variations.

(iv) Geographical isolation: It is caused by mountain ranges, rivers etc. Geographical isolation leads to reproductive isolation due to which there is no flow of genes between separated groups of the population.

Evolution and Classification

Both evolution and classification are interlinked.

→ Classification of species is a reflection of their evolutionary relationship.

→ The more characteristics two species have in common the more closely they are related.

→ The more closely they are related, the more recently they have a common ancestor.

→ Similarities among organisms allow us to group them together and to study their characteristic.

Evidence of Evolution

(i) Homologous Organs (Morphological and anatomical evidence).

→ These are the organs that have the same basic structural plan and origin but different functions.

→ Homologous organs provide evidence for evolution by telling us that they are derived from the same ancestor.

Example:

Forelimb of horse (Running)

Winds of bat (Flying)

Paw of a cat (Walk/scratch/attack)

Same basic structural plan, but different functions perform.

(ii) Analogous Organs: These are the organs that have different origin and structural plan but same function.

→ Analogous organs provide mechanism for evolution.

Example:

Wings of bat → Elongated fingers with skin folds

Wings of bird → Feathery covering along the arm

→ Different basic structure, but perform similar function i.e., flight.

(iii) Fossils: (Paleontological evidences)

→ The remains and relics of dead organisms of the past. They have preserved traces of living organisms.

→ Fossil Archaeopteryx possesses features of reptiles as well as birds. This suggests that birds have evolved from reptiles. Example:

Ammonite: Fossil-invertebrate

Trilobite: Fossil-invertebrate

Knightia: Fossil-fish

Rajasaurus: Fossil-dinosaur skull

Detecting the ratios of difference of the same element in the fossil material Radiocarbon dating [C-(14) dating]

Human Evolution

Excavating, Time dating, Fossils and the Determination of DNA sequences are the tools to study Human evolutionary relationships.

→ Although there is a great diversity of human forms all over the world, all humans are a single species.

→ All humans come from Africa. The earliest members of the human species, Homo sapiens, can be traced there. Our genetic footprints can be traced back to our African roots.

→ The residents spread across Africa, the migrants slowly spread across the planet from Africa to West Asia, then to Central Asia, Eurasia, South Asia, East Asia. They travelled down the islands of Indonesia and the Philippines to Australia, and they crossed the Bering land bridge to the Americas.

→ They did not go in a single line.

MOST IMPORTANT QUESTIONS

Q1. Which one of the following pairs are homologous organs?

(a) Forelimbs of a bird and wings of a bat.

(b) Wings of a bird and wings of a butterfly.

(c) Pectoral fins of a fish and forelimbs of a horse.

(d) Wings of a bat and wings of a cockroach.

Q2. A cross between a tall pea-plant (TT) and a short pea-plant (tt) resulted in progenies that were all tall plants because

(a) tallness is the recessive trait.

(b) shortness is the dominant trait.

(c) height of pea-plant is not governed by gene T or t.

(d) tallness is the dominant trait.

Q3. The number of pairs of sex chromosomes in the zygote of a human being is

(a) 2 (b) 3 (c) 1 (d) 4

Q4. Which of the following decides the sex of the child?

(a) male gamete, i.e., sperm (b) female gamete, i.e., ovum

(c) both sperm and ovum (d) mother

Q5. A cross between two individuals results in a ratio of 9 : 3 : 3 :1 for four possible phenotypes of progeny. This is an example of a

(a) Monohybrid cross (b) Dihybrid cross

(c) Test cross (d) F1 generation

Q6. Human offspring's sex is determined

(a) through father's sex chromosomes. (b) through mother's sex chromosomes.

(c) by hormones. (d) by enzymes.

Q7. Natural selection is called 'survival of the fittest'. Which of the following statements best describes an organism?

(a) How strong it is compared to other individuals of the same species.

(b) How much food and resources it is able to gather for its offspring.

(c) The ability to adapt to the environment in the niche it occupies.

(d) The number of fertile offspring it has

Q8. The process by which new species develop from the existing species is known as

(a) Evolution (b) Natural selection

(c) Artificial selection (d) Speciation

Q9. A cross between two individuals results in a ratio of 9 : 3 : 3 :1 for four possible phenotypes of progeny. This is an example of a

(a) Monohybrid cross (b) Dihybrid cross

(c) Test cross (d) F1 generation

Q10. Those organs which have the same basic structure but different functions are called

(a) Vestigial organs (b) Analogous organs

(c) Homologous organs (d) None of these

Q11. The number of pairs of sex chromosomes in the zygote of a human being is

(a) 2 (b) 3 (c) 1 (d) 4

Q12. Which of the following characters can be acquired but not inherited?

(a) Colour of skin (b) Size of body (c) Colour of eyes (d) Texture of hair

Q13. The genetic constitution of an organism is called.

(a) Genotype (b) phenotype (c) variation (d) gene.

Q14. Which of the following decides the sex of the child?

(a) male gamete, i.e., sperm (b) female gamete, i.e., ovum

(c) both sperm and ovum (d) mother

Q15. A zygote which has an X-chromosome inherited from the father will develop into a

(a) girl (b) boy

(c) either boy or girl (d) X-chromosome does not influence the sex of a child.

Q16. What is Heredity?

Q17. What is a gene? [Delhi]

Q18. Define 'evolution'. Describe Darwin's theory of evolution. [All India]

Q19. Give one example of each of the characters that are inherited and the ones that are acquired in humans. Mention the difference between the inherited and the acquired characters. [Delhi]

Answers:

1	2	3	4	5	6	7	8	9	10	11	12	13	14	15
A	B	C	A	B	A	C	D	B	C	C	B	A	A	A

Ans 16. It refers to the transmission of characters or traits from the parent to their offspring.

Ans 17. Gene is the unit of inheritance. Gene is the part of a chromosome which controls the appearance of a set of hereditary characteristics.

Ans 18. Evolution is the sequence of gradual changes which take place in the primitive organisms over millions of years and new species are produced. Since, the evolution is of the living organisms, so it is called 'Organic Evolution'.

Darwin's theory of Evolution: Charles Robert Darwin gave the theory of evolution in his famous book, 'The Origin of Species'. The theory of evolution proposed by Darwin is known as 'The Theory of Natural Selection'. It is also called 'Darwinism'.

According to Darwin's theory of evolution:

1. There is natural variation within any population and some individuals have more favourable variations than others.
2. Population remains fairly constant even though all species produce a large number of off springs.
3. This is due to 'competition' or struggle for existence between same and different species.
4. The struggle for survival within population eliminates the unfit individuals and those with 'favourable variations' survive and pass on these variations to their progeny to continue. This is called natural selection.
5. The favourable variations are accumulated over a long time period leading to the origin of a new species.

Ans 19. Eye colour or hair colour of a person is an example of inherited character whereas, body weight is an example of acquired character.

The basic difference between inherited and acquired character is that inherited character is passed on from parent to offspring and acquired characters are acquired by an individual during his lifetime depending upon his lifestyle.

V

Electricity

Chapter - 12

Electric Current & Circuit

Electric Current: The flow of electric charge is known as electric current. Electric current is carried by moving electrons through a conductor.

By convention, electric current flows in opposite direction to the movement of electrons.

Electric Circuit: Electric circuit is a continuous and closed path of electric current.

Expression of Electric Current: Electric current is denoted by letter 'I'. Electric current is expressed by the rate of flow of electric charges. Rate of flow means the amount of charge flowing through a particular area in unit time.

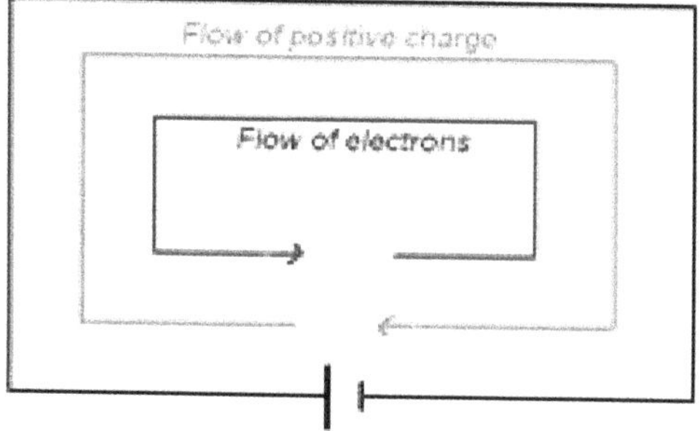

Fig: Conventional Flow of Electric Charge

If a net electric charge (Q) flows through a cross section of conductor in time t, then;

Electric Current(I)=Net charge(Q)Time(t)Electric Current(I)=Net charge(Q)Time(t)

Or, I=Q/t

Where,I is electric current,Q is net charge and t is time in second.

SI unit of Electric Charge and Current:

SI unit of electric charge is coulomb (C).

One coulomb is nearly equal to 6×10186×1018 electrons. SI unit of electric current is ampere (A). Ampere is the flow of electric charges through a surface at the rate of one coulomb per second. This means if 1 coulomb of electric charge flows through a cross-section for 1 second, it would be equal to 1 ampere.

Therefore; 1A=1C/1s

→ Charge on 1 electron = Negative charge of 1.6×10^{-19} C

i.e. Q = ne

Where, Q = Charge (total)

n = No. of electrons

e = Charge on 1 electron

A small quantity of Electric Current: Small quantity of electric current is expressed in milliampere and microampere. Milliampere is written as mA and microampere as μA

1mA (milliampere)=10^{-3}=10^{-3} A

1μA(microampere)=10^{-6}=10^{-6} A

Ammeter: An apparatus to measure electric current in a circuit.

Electric Potential and Potential Difference

Electric Potential: The amount of electric potential energy at a point is called electric potential.

Electric Potential difference: The difference in the amount of electric potential energy between two points in an electric circuit is called ELECTRIC POTENTIAL DIFFERENCE.

Electric potential difference is known as voltage, which is equal to the work done per unit charge to move the charge between two points against the static electric field.

$$\text{Voltage} = \frac{\text{Work done}}{\text{Charge}}$$

Voltage or electric potential difference is denoted by 'V'. Therefore;

$$V = \frac{W}{Q} \text{ -----------(1)}$$

Where, W = work done and Q = Charge

Electric Potential

SI unit of electric potential difference is volt and denoted by 'V'. This is named in honor of Italian physicist **Alessandro Volta**.

Voltmeter: An apparatus to measure the potential difference or electric potential difference between two points in an electric circuit.

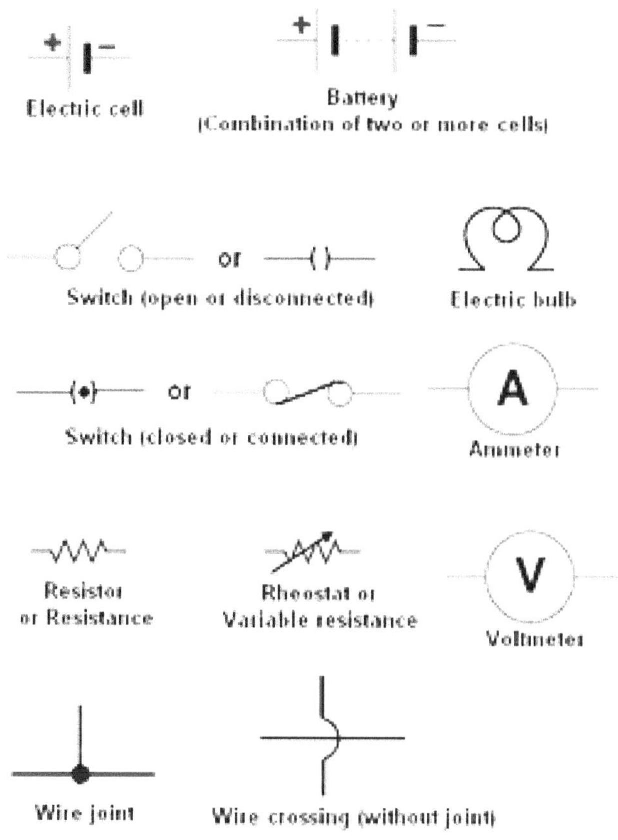

Important Symbols

Ohm's Law

The potential difference across the two points of a metallic conductor is directly proportional to the current passing through the circuit provided that temperature remains constant.

- Mathematical expression for Ohm's law

$V \propto I$

$V = IR$

R is a constant called resistance for a given metal

V-I graph for Ohm's law

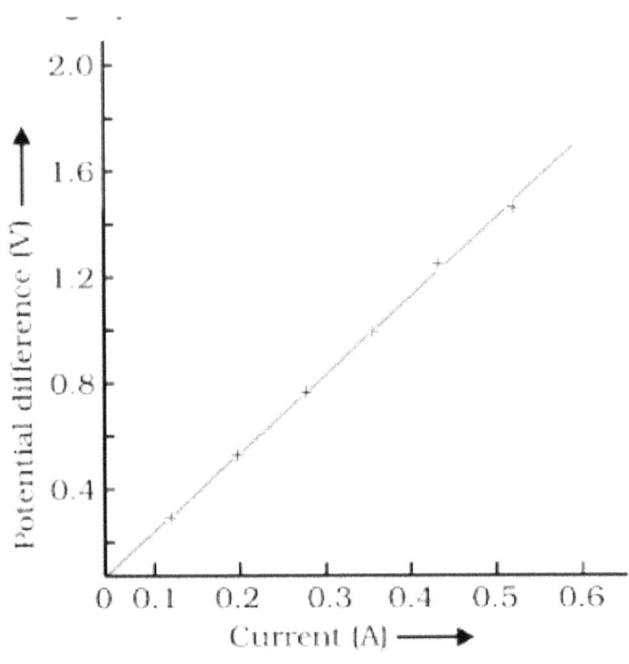

V-I Graph

Resistance (R): It is the property of a conductor to resist the flow of charges through it. Ohm (Ω): S. I. unit of resistance.
1 ohm = 1 volt/1ampere
When a potential difference is 1 V and the current through the circuit is 1 A, then resistance is 1 ohm.
Rheostat: Variable resistance is a component used to regulate current without changing the source of voltage.

Resistance

Resistance is a property of conductor due to which it resists the flow of electric current through it. The component that is used to resist the flow of electric current in a circuit is called a resistor.

In practical applications, resistors are used to increase or decrease the electric current.

Variable Resistance: The component of an electric circuit which is used to regulate the current; without changing the voltage from the source; is called variable resistance.

Rheostat: This is a device that is used in a circuit to provide variable resistance.

Cause of Resistance in a Conductor:

The flow of electrons in a conductor is an electric current. The particles of the conductor create a hindrance to the flow of electrons; because of attraction between them. This hindrance is the cause of resistance in the flow of electricity.

Resistance in a conductor depends on the nature, length, and area of the cross-section of the conductor.

Nature of material: Some materials create the least hindrance and hence are called good conductors. Silver is the best conductor of electricity. While some other materials create more hindrance in the flow of electric current, i.e. flow of electrons through them. Such materials are called bad conductors. Bad conductors are also known as insulators. Hard plastic is one of the best insulators of electricity.

Length of conductor: Resistance R is directly proportional to the length of the conductor. This means Resistance increases with an increase in the length of the conductor. This is the cause why long electric wires create more resistance to the electric current.

Thus, Resistance (R) $\propto$ length of conductor (l)

or $R \propto l$ --------(i)

Area of cross-section: Resistance R is inversely proportional to the area of cross-section (A) of the conductor. This means R will decrease with an increase in the area of conductor and vice versa. More area of conductor facilitates the flow of electric current through more area and thus decreases the resistance. This is the cause that thick copper wire creates less resistance to the electric current.

Thus, resistance$\propto$1Area of a cross-section of the conductor (A)

Or, $R \propto A$ ---------(ii)

From equation (i) and (ii)

$R \propto lA$

$$RA = \rho l$$

$$\text{Or, } \rho = \frac{RA}{l} \text{ ---------(iv)}$$

Where ρ (rho) is the proportionality constant. It is called the electrical resistivity of the material of conductors.

The SI unit of resistivity: Since, the SI unit of R is Ω, the SI unit of Area is m^2 and the SI unit of length is m. Hence

Thus, the SI unit of resistivity (ρ) is Ω m

Resistivity (P): It is defined as the resistance offered by a cube of a material of side 1m when current flows perpendicular to its opposite faces

Materials having a resistivity in the range of 10^{-8} Ω m to 10^{-6} Ω m are considered very good conductors. Silver has resistivity equal to 1.60 X 10^{-8} Ω m and copper has resistivity equal to 1.62 X 10^{-8} Ω m.

Rubber and glass are very good insulators. They have a resistivity in the order of 10^{12} Ω m to 10^{17} Ω m.

The resistivity of materials varies with temperature. Resistance Of A System of Resistors:

Alloys do not oxidize (burn) readily at high temperatures, so they are commonly used in electrical heating devices.

Copper and aluminum are used for electrical transmission lines as they have low resistivity.

Resistors are joined in two ways, i.e. in series and in parallel.

Resistors in Series: When resistors are joined from end to end, it is called in series. In this case, the total resistance of the system is equal to the sum of the resistance of all the resistors in the system.

Let total resistance = R

Resistance of resistors are R_1, R_2, R_3, ... R_n

Therefore, $R = R_1 + R_2 + R_3 + \dots\dots\dots\dots + R_n$

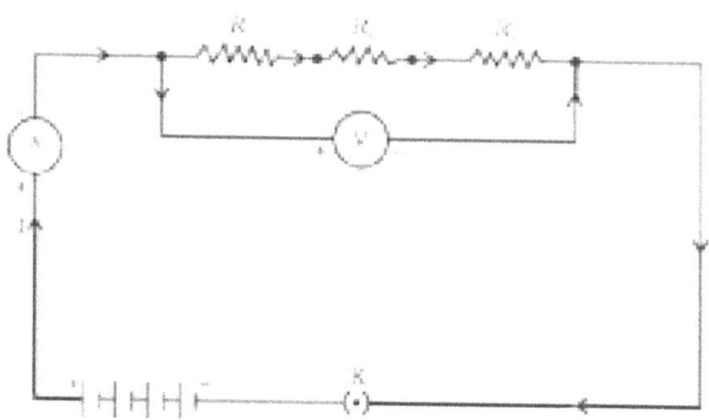

Resistor in Series Combination

Current through each resistor is the same.

The equivalent resistance is larger than the largest individual resistance.

Total voltage = Sum of voltage drops

$V = V1 + V2 + V3$

Voltage across each resistor

$V1 = IR1$

$V2 = IR2$ [$V1 + V2 + V3 = V$]

$V3 = IR3V = IR$

$V = IR1 + IR2 + IR3$

$IR = I(R1 + R2 + R3)$

$R = R1 + R2 + R3$

Resistors in parallel: When resistors are joined in parallel, the reciprocal of the total resistance of the system is equal to the sum of the reciprocal of the resistance of resistors.

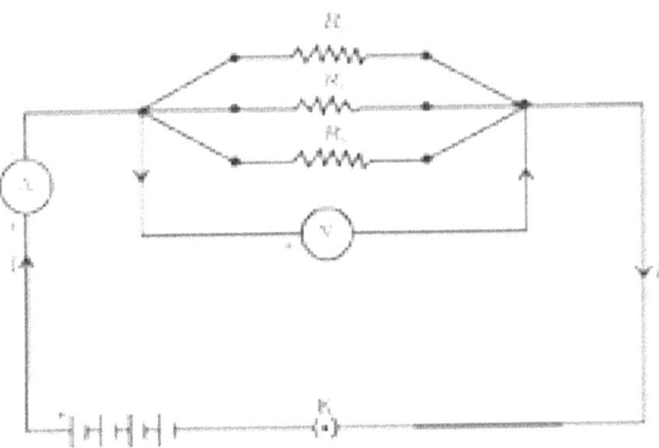

Resistors in parallel

Let total resistance = R

Resistance of resistors are R_1, R_2, R_3, ... R_n

The voltage across each resistor is the same and equal to the applied voltage. The total current is equal to the sum of currents through the individual resistances.

I = I1 + I2 + I3

⇒ V/R = V/R1 + V/R2 + V/R3

The reciprocal of equivalent resistance is equal to the sum of reciprocals of individual resistances.

1/Rp = 1/R1 + 1/R2 + 1/R3

$$\frac{1}{R} = \frac{1}{R_1} + \frac{1}{R_2} + \frac{1}{R_3} + \ldots\ldots + \frac{1}{R_n}$$

Resistors in parallel

Advantages of Parallel Combination over Series Combination

(i) In a series circuit, when one component fails, the circuit is broken and none of the components works.

(ii) Different appliances have different requirements of current. This cannot be satisfied in series as the current remains same.

(iii) The total resistance in a parallel circuit is decreased

Heating Effect of Electric Current

When an electric current is supplied to a purely resistive conductor, the energy of the electric current is dissipated entirely in the form of heat and as a result, the resistor gets heated. The heating of resistor because of dissipation of electrical energy is commonly known as the Heating Effect of Electric Current. Some examples are as follows:

When electric energy is supplied to an electric bulb, the filament gets heated because of which it gives light. The heating of an electric bulb happens because of the heating effect of the electric current.

When an electric iron is connected to an electric circuit, the element of electric iron gets heated because of the dissipation of electric energy, which heats the electric iron. The element of an electric iron is a purely resistive conductor. This happens because of the heating effect of the electric current.

Cause of heating effect of electric current: Electric current generates heat to overcome the resistance offered by the conductor through which it passes. Higher the resistance, the electric current will generate a higher amount of heat. Thus, the generation of heat by electric current while passing through a conductor is an inevitable consequence. This heating effect is used in many appliances, such as electric iron, electric heater, electric geyser, etc.

Joule's Law of Heating:

Let; an electric current I is flowing through a resistor having a resistance equal to R.

The potential difference through the resistor is equal to V.

The charge Q flows through the circuit for the time t.

Thus, work done in moving of charge Q of potential difference V=VQ

Since this charge Q flows through the circuit for time t

Therefore; power input (P) to the circuit can be given by the following equation:

$$P = V \times \frac{Q}{t}\text{--------(1)}$$

We know, electric current $I = \frac{Q}{t}$

Substituting $\frac{Q}{t} = I$ in equation (i), we get;

$$P = VI\text{..........(ii)}$$

Since the electric energy is supplied for time t, thus after multiplying both sides of equation (ii) by time t, we get

$P \times t = VI \times t = VIt$ .....(iii)

Thus, for steady current, I, the heat produced (H) in time t is equal to VIt

Or, $H = VIt$ ....(iv)

We know; according to Ohm's law; $V = IR$

By substituting this value of V in equation (iv), we get;

$H = IR \times It$

Or, $H = I^2Rt$ ....(v)

The expression (v) is known as Joule's Law of Heating, which states that heat produced in a resistor is directly proportional to the square of current given to the resistor, directly proportional to the resistance for a given current, and directly proportional to the time for which the current is flowing through the resistor.

Heating Effect of Electric Current Practical Application

Practical Application of Heating Effect of Electric Current & Electric Power

For exploiting the heating effect of electric current, the element of appliances must have a high melting point to retain more heat. The heating effect of electric current is used in the following applications:

Electric Bulb: In an electric bulb, the filament of the bulb gives light because of the heating effect of electricity. The filament of the bulb is generally made of tungsten metal; having melting point equal to 3380°C.

Electric iron: The element of an electric iron is made of alloys having a high melting point. Electric heater and geyser work on the same mechanism.

Electric fuse: Electric fuse is used to protect the electric appliances from high voltage; if any. An electric fuse is made of metal or alloy of metals, such as aluminums, copper, iron, lead, etc. In the case of flow of higher voltage than specified, fuse wire melts and protects the electric appliances.

The fuse of 1A, 2A, 3A, 5A, 10A, etc. is used for domestic purposes.

Suppose, if an electric heater consumes 1000W at 220V.

Then electric current in circuit I=P/V

Or, I=1000W–220V=4.5AI=1000W–220V=4.5A

Thus, in this case, a fuse of 5A should be used to protect the electric heater in the case of flow of higher voltage.

Electric Power:

SI unit of electric power is the watt (W).

1W=1volt×1ampere=1V×1A1W=1volt×1ampere=1V×1A

1 kilo watt or 1kW = 1000 W

Consumption of electricity (electric energy) is generally measured in kilowatt.

Unit of electric energy is kilowatt-hour (kWh)

1kWh=1000watt×1hour=1000W×3600s

Or, $1kWh=3.6\times10^{6}$watt second$=3.6\times10^{6}$ J

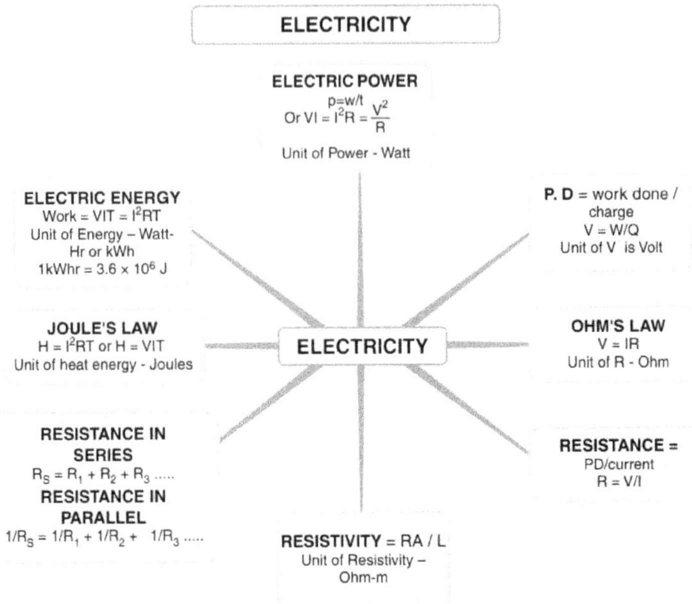

Flow Chart

MOST IMPORTANT QUESTIONS

Q1. A boy records that 4000 joules of work is required to transfer 10 coulombs of charge between two points of a resistor of 50 Ω. The current passing through it is

(a) 2 A (b) 4 A (c) 8 A (d) 16 A

Q2. Two wires of the same length and area made of two materials of resistivity ρ_1 and ρ_2 are connected in series to a source of potential V. The equivalent resistivity for the same area is

(a) $\rho_1 + \rho_2$ (b) $\dfrac{\rho_1 \rho_2}{\rho_1 + \rho_2}$

(c) $\dfrac{(\rho_1 + \rho_2)}{\rho_1 \rho_2}$ (d) $\left(\dfrac{|\rho_1 + \rho_2|}{2}\right)$

Q3. Calculate the current flows through the 10 Ω resistor in the following circuit.

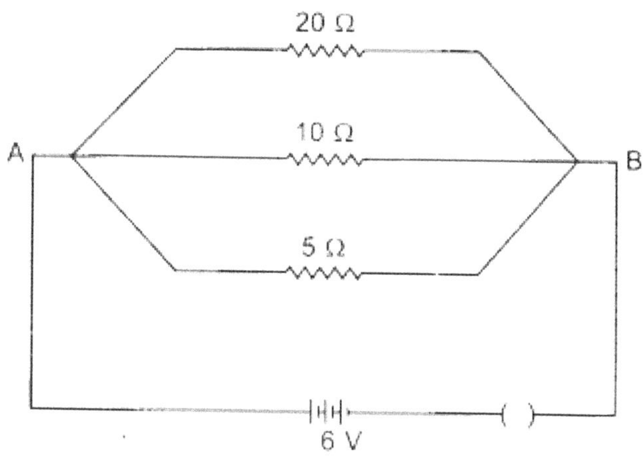

(a) 1.2 A (b) 0.6 A (c) 0.2 A (d) 2.0 A

Q4. A fuse wire repeatedly gets burnt when used with a good heater. It is advised to use a fuse wire of

(a) more length (b) less radius (c) less length (d) more radius

Q5. The effective resistance between A and B is

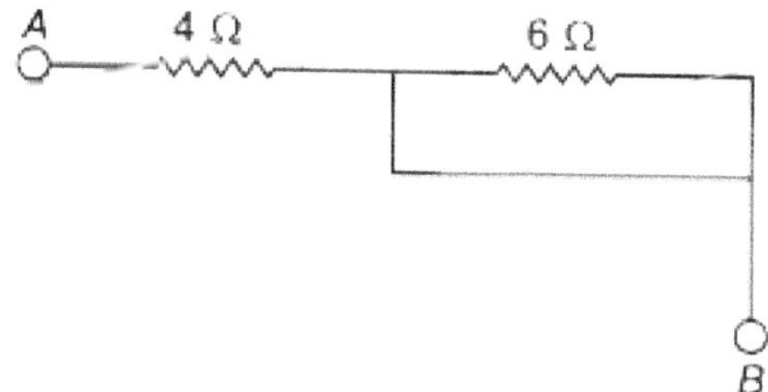

(a) 4Ω (b) 6Ω (c) May be 10 Ω (d) Must be 10 Ω

Q6. If the current I through a resistor is increased by 100 % (assume that temperature remains unchanged), the increase in power dissipated will be [NCERT Exemplar Problems]

(a) 100% (b) 200% (c) 300 % (d) 400 %

Q7. The resistivity does not change if [NCERT Exemplar Problems]
(a) the material is changed (b) the temperature is changed
(c) the shape of the resistor is changed (d) both material and temperature are changed

Q8. Two devices are connected between two points say A and B in parallel. The physical quantity that will remain the same between the two points is
(a) current (b) voltage (c) resistance (d) None of these

Q9. 100 J of heat is produced each second in a 4Ω resistor. The potential difference across the resistor will be:
(a) 30 V (b) 10 V (c) 20 V (d) 25 V

Q10. An electric bulb is connected to a 220V generator. The current is 0.50 A. What is the power of the bulb?
(a) 440 W (b) 110 W (c) 55 W (d) 0.0023 W

Q11. The electrical resistance of insulators is
(a) high (b) low (c) zero (d) infinitely high

Q12. Coulomb is the SI unit of:
(a) charge (b) current
(c) potential difference (d) resistance

Q13. The resistivity of a metallic wise depends on
(a) its length (b) its shape (c) its thickness (d) nature of the material

Q14. What is the commercial unit of electrical energy?
(a) Joules (b) Kilojoules (c) Kilowatt-hour (d) Watt-hour

Q15. A boy records that 4000 joules of work is required to transfer 10 coulomb of charge between two points of a resistor of 50 Ω. The current passing through it is
(a) 2 A (b) 4 A (c) 8 A (d) 16 A

Q16. What happens to the resistance of a conductor when its area of cross-section is increased? [CBSE 2011]

Q17. A given length of a wire is doubled on itself and this process is repeated once again. By what factor does the resistance of the wire change? [CBSE 2011]

Q18. Fill in the Blanks

1. The SI unit of current is ....
2. According to .... Law, the potential difference across the ends of a resistor is directly proportional to the .... through it, provided its remains constant.
3. The resistance of a conductor depends directly on its .... , inversely on its .... and also on the .... of the conductor.

4. The SI unit of resistivity is ....
5. If the potential difference across the ends of a conductor is doubled, the current flowing through it, gets ....

Q19. Find the current drawn from the battery by the network of four resistors Shown in the figure.

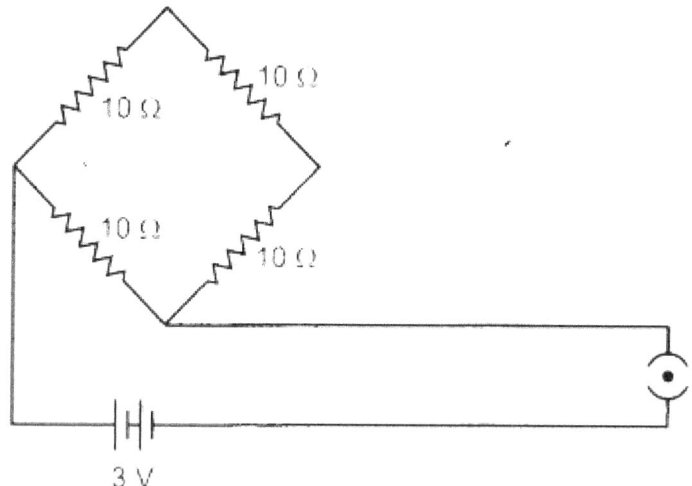

Q20. Two wires A and B are of equal length and have equal resistance. If the resistivity of A is more than that of B which wire is thicker and why? For the electric circuit given below calculate:

(i) Current in each resistor,

(ii) Total current drawn from the battery, and(iii) Equivalent resistance of the Circuit

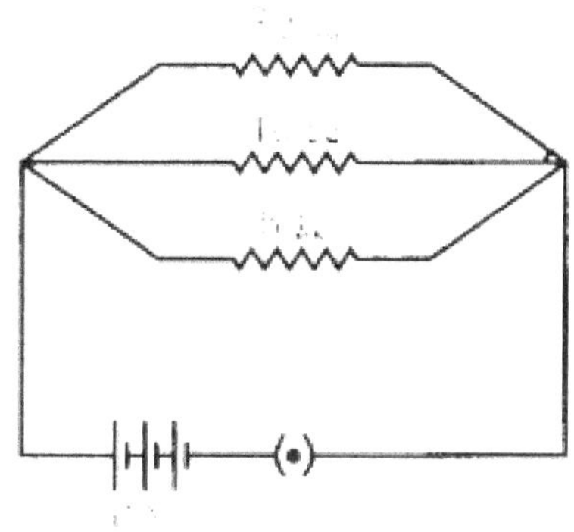

Q21. (a) Define electric power. Express it in terms of potential difference V and resistance R. (b) An electrical fuse is rated at 2 A. What is meant by this statement?
(c) An electric iron of 1 kW is operated at 220 V. Find which of the following fuses that respectively rated at 1 A,3 A and 5 A can be used in it.

Answers:

1	2	3	4	5	6	7	8	9	10	11	12	13	14	15
C	A	B	D	A	C	C	B	B	B	D	D	C	C	

Ans 16. On **increasing** the **area of cross-section**, **resistance** decreases. This is because **resistance** is inversely proportional to **area.**

Ans 17. Length becomes one-fourth of the original length and area of cross-section becomes four times that of the original.

i.e., $$l_2 = \frac{1}{4}l_1 \text{ and } A_2 = 4A_1$$

$\therefore$ $$\frac{R_2}{R_1} = \frac{l_2}{l_1} \times \frac{A_1}{A_2} = \frac{1}{4} \times \frac{1}{4} = \frac{1}{16}$$

$\Rightarrow$ $$R_2 = \frac{1}{16}R_1$$

So, new resistance is $\left(\frac{1}{16}\right)$th of original resistance.

Ans 18. 1. ampere
2. Ohm's, current, temperature
3. length, area of cross-section, material
4. ohm-meter (Ω m)
5. Doubled

Ans 19.

Equivalent resistance the given network is

$$\frac{1}{R} = \frac{1}{R_4} + \frac{1}{R_1 + R_2 + R_3}$$

$$= \frac{1}{10} + \frac{1}{10+10+10} = \frac{1}{10} + \frac{1}{30} = \frac{3+1}{30} = \frac{4}{30}$$

$$\therefore \quad R = \frac{30}{4} = 7.5\ \Omega$$

Current drawn from the battery

$$I = \frac{V}{R} = \frac{3}{7.5} = \frac{30}{75} = \frac{2}{5}$$

$$\Rightarrow \quad I = 0.4\ \text{A}$$

Ans 20.

Using, $$R = \rho \frac{l}{A}$$

$$\Rightarrow \quad \frac{\rho}{A} = \frac{R}{l} = \text{Constant} = K \text{ (for same } l \text{ and } R)$$

$$\Rightarrow \quad \rho = kA$$

$$\Rightarrow \quad \rho \propto A$$

So, for different materials having the same resistance per unit length, greater resistivity material wire has a more cross-sectional area.
Hence, wire A is thicker than that of B.
(i) Current through each resistor

$$I_1 = \frac{V}{R_1} = \frac{6}{5} = 1.2\ \text{A}$$

$$I_2 = \frac{V}{R_2} = \frac{6}{10} = 0.6\ \text{A}$$

$$I_3 = \frac{V}{R_3} = \frac{6}{30} = 0.2\ \text{A}$$

Current in 5 Ω, 10 Ω and 30 Ω are therefore, 1.2 A, 0.6 A and 0.2 A respectively.

(*ii*) Total current drawn from the battery

$$I = I_1 + I_2 + I_3 = 1.2 + 0.6 + 0.2 = 2.0 \text{ A}$$

(*iii*) $R_1 = 5\ \Omega$, $R_2 = 10\ \Omega$ and $R_3 = 30\ \Omega$ are connected in parallel. So their equivalent resistance

$$\frac{1}{R} = \frac{1}{R_1} + \frac{1}{R_2} + \frac{1}{R_3} = \frac{1}{5} + \frac{1}{10} + \frac{1}{30} = \frac{1}{3}$$

$$R = 3\ \Omega$$

Ans 21. (a) Electric power: It is the rate of doing work by an energy source or the rate at which the electrical energy is dissipated or consumed per unit time in the electric circuit is called electric power.

So, $$\text{Power } P = \frac{\text{Work done } (w)}{\text{Time } (t)}$$

$$= \frac{\text{Electrical energy dissipated}}{\text{Time } (t)}$$

$$= VI = \frac{V^2}{R}$$

(b) It means, the maximum current that will flow through it is only 2 A. Fuse wire will melt if the current exceeds 2 A value through it.

(*c*) Given: $P = 1 \text{ kW} = 1000 \text{ W}$, $V = 220 \text{ V}$

Current drawn, $$I = \frac{P}{V} = \frac{1000}{220} = \frac{50}{11} = 4.54 \text{ A}$$

To run electric iron of 1 kW, rated fuse of 5 A should be used.

VI

Magnetic effects of current

Chapter - 13

Magnetic Effect of Electric Current

Properties of magnet:

- A free suspended magnet always points towards the north and south directions.
- The pole of a magnet that points toward the north direction is called the north pole or north seeking.
- The pole of a magnet that points toward the south direction is called the south pole or south seeking.
- Like poles of magnets repel each other while unlike poles of magnets attract each other.

Similar to other effects; electric current also produces a magnetic effect. The magnetic effect of electric current is known as an electromagnetic effect.

It is observed that when a compass is brought near a current-carrying conductor the needle of the compass gets deflected because of the flow of electricity. This shows that electric current produces a magnetic effect.

Magnetic field and Field Lines

The influence of force surrounding a magnet is called a magnetic field. In the magnetic field, the force exerted by a magnet can be detected using a compass or any other magnet.

The imaginary lines of the magnetic field around a magnet are called field lines or field lines of magnets. When iron fillings are allowed to settle around a bar magnet, they get arranged in a pattern that mimics the magnetic field lines. The Fieldline of a magnet can also be detected using a compass. The magnetic field is a vector quantity, i.e. it has both direction and magnitude.

The direction of Field Line: Outside the magnet, the direction of the magnetic field line is taken from the north pole to the South Pole. Inside the magnet, the direction of the magnetic field line is taken from the south pole to the north pole.

Strength of magnetic field: The closeness of field lines shows the relative strength of the magnetic field, i.e. closer lines show stronger magnetic field and vice-versa. Crowded field lines near the poles of the magnet show more strength.

Magnetic field Due to a Current-Carrying Conductor:

Magnetic field due to current through a straight conductor:

A current-carrying straight conductor has a magnetic field in the form of concentric circles; around it. The magnetic field of the current-carrying straight conductor can be shown by magnetic field lines.

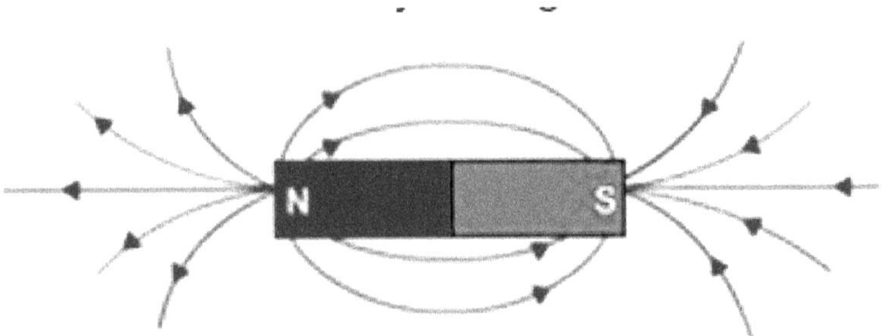

Fig: Magnetic Field Lines

The imaginary lines of the magnetic field around a magnet are called field lines or field line of magnet. When iron fillings are allowed to settle around a bar magnet, they get arranged in a pattern that mimics the magnetic field lines. The Fieldline of a magnet can also be detected using a compass. The magnetic field is a vector quantity, i.e. it has both direction and magnitude.

The direction of Field Line: Outside the magnet, the direction of the magnetic field line is taken from north pole to South Pole. Inside the magnet, the direction of the magnetic field line is taken from south pole to north pole.

Strength of magnetic field: The closeness of field lines shows the relative strength of the magnetic field, i.e. closer lines show a stronger magnetic field and vice-versa. Crowded field lines near the poles of magnet show more strength.

Right-Hand Thumb Rule:

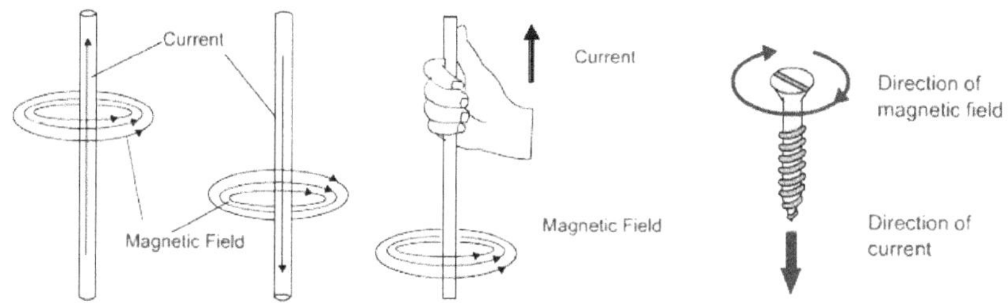

Right-Hand Rule

The direction of the magnetic field; in relation to the direction of electric current through a straight conductor can be depicted by using the Right-Hand Thumb Rule. It is also known as Maxwell's Corkscrew Rule.

If a current-carrying conductor is held by the right hand; keeping the thumb straight and if the direction of electric current is in the direction of the thumb, then the direction of wrapping of other fingers will show the direction of a magnetic field.

As per Maxwell's corkscrew rule, if the direction of forwarding movement of the screw shows the direction of the current, then the direction of rotation of the screw shows the direction of the magnetic field.

Properties of Magnetic Field:

- The magnitude; of the magnetic field increases with an increase in electric current and decreases with a decrease in electric current.
- The magnitude of a magnetic field; produced by electric current; decreases with an increase in distance and vice-versa. The size of concentric circles of magnetic field lines increases with distance from the conductor, which shows that the magnetic field decreases with distance.
- Magnetic field lines are always parallel to each other.
- No two field lines cross each other.

Magnetic field due to current through a circular loop

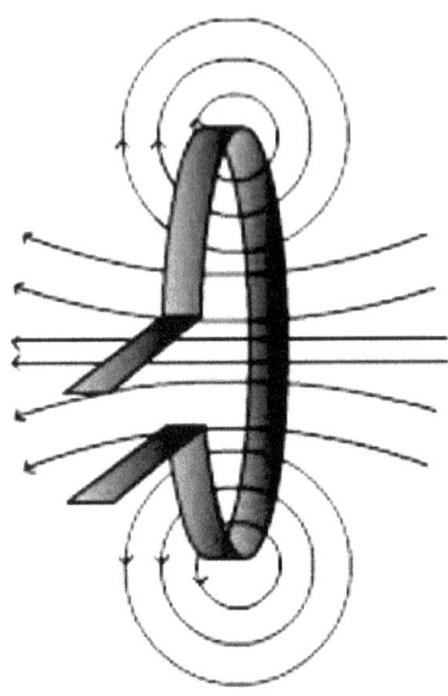

In the case of a circular current-carrying conductor, the magnetic field is produced in the same manner as it is in the case of a straight current-carrying conductor.

In the case of a circular current-carrying conductor, the magnetic field lines would be in the form of concentric circles around every part of the periphery of the conductor. Since, magnetic field lines tend to remain closed when near the conductor, the magnetic field would be stronger near the periphery of the loop. On the other hand, the magnetic field lines would be distant from each other when we move towards the center of the current-carrying loop. Finally; at the center, the arcs of big circles would appear as a straight line.

The direction of the magnetic field can be identified using Right Hand Thumb's Rule. Let us assume that the current is moving in an anti-clockwise direction in the loop. In that case, the magnetic field would be in a clockwise direction; at the top of the loop. Moreover, it would be in an anticlockwise direction at the bottom of the loop.

Clock Face Rule: A current-carrying loop works like a disc magnet. The polarity of this magnet can be easily understood with the help of the clock face rule. If the current is flowing in an anti-clockwise direction, then the face of the loop shows the north pole. On the other hand, if the current is flowing in a clockwise direction, then the face of the loop shows the south pole.

Magnetic field and number of turns of coil: The magnitude of the magnetic field gets summed up with the increase in the number of turns of the coil. If there are 'n' turns of the coil, the magnitude of the magnetic field will be 'n' times of magnetic field in case of a single turn of the coil.

Magnetic Field due to a current in a Solenoid:

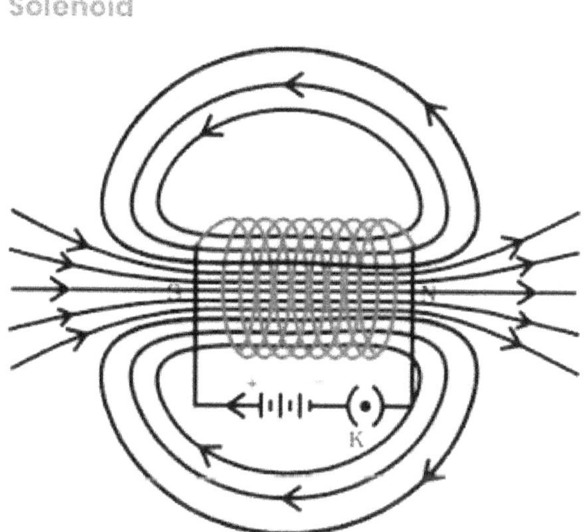

Field lines of the magnetic field through and around a current carrying solenoid.

The solenoid is the coil with many circular turns of insulated copper wire wrapped closely in the shape of a cylinder.

(i) Outside the solenoid: North to South

(ii) Inside the solenoid: South to North

A current-carrying solenoid produces a similar pattern of the magnetic field as a bar magnet. One end of the solenoid behaves as the north pole and another end behaves as the south pole. Magnetic field lines are parallel inside the solenoid; similar to a bar magnet; which shows that the magnetic field is the same at all points inside the solenoid.

By producing a strong magnetic field inside the solenoid, magnetic materials can be magnetized. Magnet formed by producing a magnetic field inside a solenoid is called an electromagnet.

Factors affecting magnetic field of a circular current carrying conductor

→ Magnetic field ∝ Current passing through the conductor

→ Magnetic ∝ 1/Distance from conductor

→ Magnetic field ∝ No. of turns in the coil

Force on a current-carrying conductor in a magnetic field:

A current-carrying conductor exerts a force when a magnet is placed in its vicinity. Similarly, a magnet also exerts equal and opposite force on the current-carrying conductor. This was suggested by Marie Ampere, a French Physicist and considered as the founder of the science of electromagnetism.

The direction of force over the conductor gets reversed with the change in direction of the flow of electric current. It is observed that the magnitude of the force is highest when the direction of current is at right angles to the magnetic field.

Electromagnet

→ It is a temporary magnet, so, can be easily demagnetized.
→ Strength can be varied.
→ Polarity can be reversed.
→ Generally strong magnet.

Permanent Magnet

→ Cannot be easily demagnetized.
→ Strength is fixed.
→ Polarity cannot be reversed.
→ Generally weak magnet.

Fleming's Left Hand Rule:

If the direction of the electric current is perpendicular to the magnetic field, the direction of force is also perpendicular to both of them. The Fleming's Left Hand Rule states that if the left hand is stretched in a way that the index finger, the middle finger, and the thumb are in mutually perpendicular directions; then the index finger and middle finger of a stretched left-hand show the direction of magnetic field and direction of electric current respectively and the thumb shows the direction of motion or force acting on the conductor. The directions of electric current, magnetic field and force are similar to three mutually perpendicular axes, i.e. x, y, and z axes.

Many devices, such as electric motor, electric generator, loudspeaker, etc. works on Fleming's left Hand Rule.

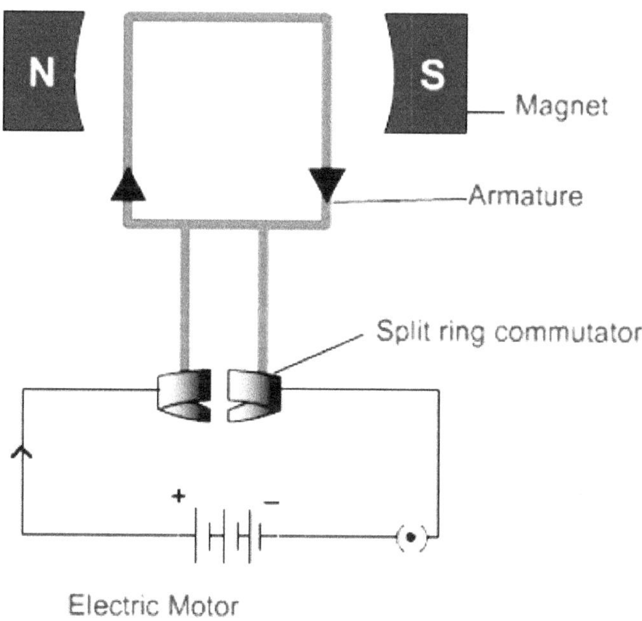

Electric Motor

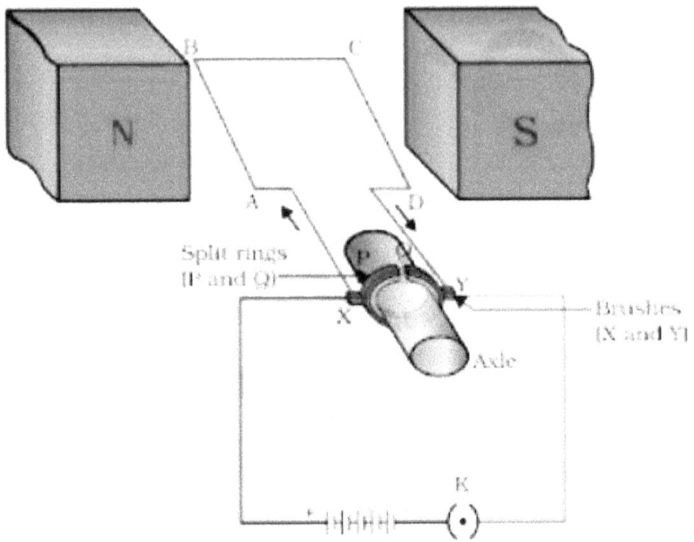

An electric motor consists of a rectangular coil ABCD of insulated copper wire. The coil is placed between the two poles of a magnetic field such that the arm AB and CD are perpendicular to the direction of the magnetic field. The ends of the coil are connected to the two halves P and Q of a split ring. The inner sides of these halves are insulated and attached to an axle. The external conducting edges of P and Q touch two conducting stationary brushes X and Y, respectively. Current in the coil ABCD enters from the source battery through conducting brush X and flows back to the battery through brush Y. The force acting on arm AB pushes it downwards while the force acting on arm CD pushes it upwards. Thus the coil and the axle O mounted free to turn about an axis, rotate anti-clockwise. At half rotation, Q makes contact with the brush X and P with brush Y. Therefore the current in the coil gets reversed and flows along the path DCBA.

The split ring acts as a commutator that reverses the direction of current and also reverses the direction of force acting on the two arms AB and CD. Thus the arm AB of the coil that was earlier pushed down is now pushed up and the arm CD previously pushed up is now pushed down. Therefore the coil and the axle rotate half a turn more in the same direction. The reversing of the current is repeated at each half rotation, giving rise to a continuous rotation of the coil and to the axle.

Commutator: A device that reverses the direction of flow of current through a circuit is called a commutator.

Armature: The soft iron core, on which the coil is wound including the coils is called an armature. It enhances the power of the motor

MRI (Magnetic Resonance Imaging): Image of internal organs of the body can be obtained using the magnetic field of the organ.

Galvanometer: Instrument that can detect the presence of current in a circuit. It also detects the direction of the current.

Commercial use of motors

(i) an electromagnet in place of a permanent magnet

(ii) large number of turns of the conducting wire in the current-carrying coil

(iii) a soft iron core on which the coil is wound.

Fleming's Right-Hand Rule

Hold the thumb, the forefinger, and the middle finger of the right hand at right angles to each other. If the forefinger is in the direction of the magnetic field and the thumb points in the direction of the motion of the conductor, then the direction of the induced current is indicated by the middle finger.

- Working principle of an electric generator.
- Used to find the direction of induced current.

Electric Generator

An electric generator, mechanical energy is used to rotate a conductor in a magnetic field to produce electricity. An electric generator consists of a rotating rectangular coil ABCD placed between the two poles of a permanent magnet. The two ends of this coil are connected to the two rings R1 and R2. The inner side of these rings are made insulated. The inner side of these rings are made insulated. The two conducting stationary brushes B1 and B2 are kept pressed separately on the rings R1 and R2, respectively. The two rings R1 and R2 are internally attached to an axle. The axle may be mechanically rotated from outside to rotate the coil inside the magnetic field. Outer ends of the two brushes are connected to the galvanometer to show the flow of current in the given external circuit. When the axle attached to the two rings is rotated such that the arm AB moves up (and the arm CD moves down) in the magnetic field produced by the permanent magnet. After half a rotation, arm CD starts moving up and AB moving down. As a result, the

directions of the induced currents in both the arms change, giving rise to

the net induced current in the direction DCBA. The current in the external circuit now flows from B1 to B2. Thus after every half rotation
the polarity of the current in the respective arms changes. To get a direct current (DC), a split-ring type commutator must be used. With this arrangement, one brush is at all times in contact with the arm moving up in the field, while the other is in contact with the arm moving down. The direct current always flows in one direction, whereas the alternating current reverses its direction periodically.

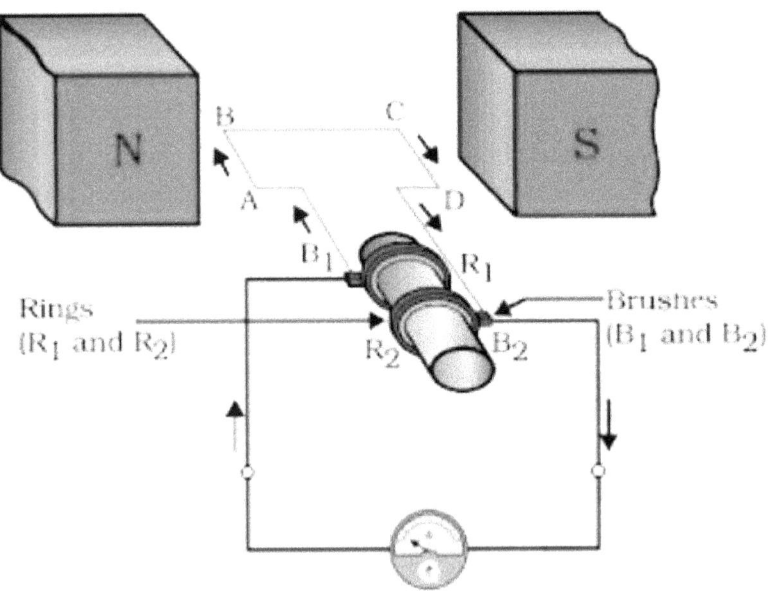

Electric Generator

Alternate Current (A. C.)

The current reverses its direction periodically. In India, A. C. reverses its direction every 1/100 second.
Time period = 1/100 + 1/100 = 1/50 s
Frequency = 1/time period = 1/50 = 50 Hz
Advantage of A.C.- A. C. can be transmitted over long distances without much loss of energy.
The disadvantage of A.C.- A. C. cannot be stored.

Direct Current (D. C.)

The current does not reverse its direction.

→ D. C. can be stored.

→ Loss of energy during transmission over long distances is high.

→ Sources of D. C.: Cell, Battery, Storage cells.

Domestic Electric Circuits

There are three kinds of wires used:

(i) Live wire (positive) with red insulation cover.

(ii) Neutral wire (negative) with black insulation cover.

(iii)Earth wire with green insulation cover.

The potential difference between live and neutral wire in India is 220 V.

Pole ⇒ Main supply ⇒ Fuse ⇒ Electricity meter ⇒ Distribution box ⇒ To separate circuits

Earth Wire: Protects us from electric shock in case of leakage of current especially in metallic body appliances. It provides a low resistance path for current in case of leakage of current.

Short Circuit: When live wire comes in direct contact with neutral wire accidentally. The resistance of the circuit becomes low which can result in overloading.

Overloading: When the current drawn is more than the current-carrying capacity of a conductor, it results in overloading.

Causes of overloading

(i) Accidental hike in voltage supply.

(ii) Use of more than one appliance in a single socket.

Safety devices

(i) Electric fuse

(ii) Earth wire

(iii) MCB (Miniature Circuit Breaker)

VII
Our Environment

Chapter - 15

Our Environment

Environment: Our surrounding is called the environment.

In this lesson, you will learn about the following:

- Ecosystem and its components
- Biotic and abiotic components.
- Food chain and food web
- Energy transfer through trophic levels
- Ozone layer and its concerns.

Ecosystem: This is a system of interdependencies among various living beings and non-living things in a given habitat.

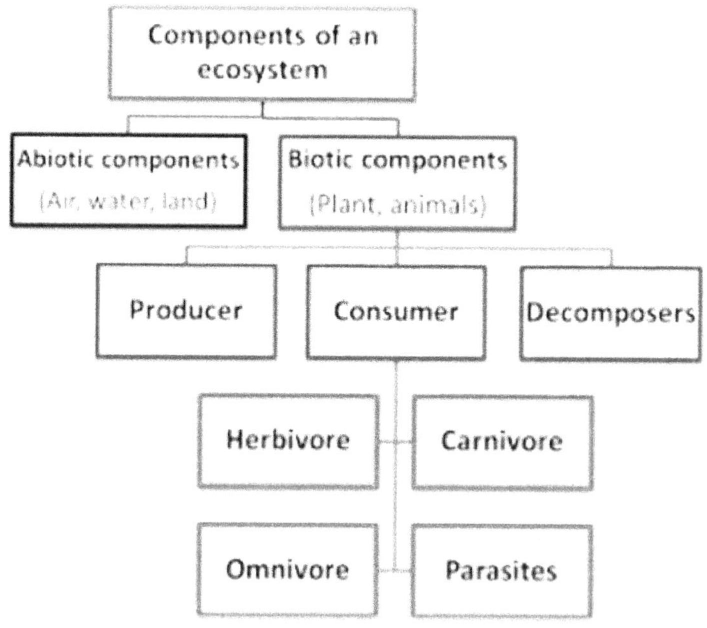

Components of an Ecosystem

An ecosystem has two types of components, viz. biotic component and abiotic component.

Abiotic Component

All the non-living things make up the abiotic component of an ecosystem. Air, water, and soil are abiotic components.

Air provides oxygen (for respiration), carbon dioxide (for photosynthesis), and other gases for various needs of living beings.

Water is essential for all living beings because all metabolic activities happen in the presence of water.

Soil is the reservoir of various nutrients which are utilized by plants. Through plants, these nutrients reach other living beings.

Biotic Component

All living beings make up the biotic component of an ecosystem.

- Green plants play the role of **producers**; because they prepare their own food.
- Animals and other living beings play the role of **consumers**; because they take food (directly or indirectly) from plants.
- Bacteria and fungi play the role of **decomposers**; as they decompose dead remains of plants and animals so that raw materials of organisms can be channelized back to the environment.

Food Chain

A food chain is a simple representation of the transfer of energy from the sun to different biotic components of an ecosystem. Sun is the ultimate source of energy. Green plants convert solar energy into chemical energy during photosynthesis. When an animal takes food, this energy is supplied to the animal and the process goes on. A simple food chain can be shown as follows:

Producer → Primary Consumer → Secondary Consumer

Food Web:

Real-life cannot be as simple as a food chain shown above. In any ecosystem, there can be many food chains that are interlinked at various levels. Thus, many food chains form a network which is called the food web.

Producers: All green plants and blue-green algae can produce their own food using abiotic components (photosynthesis), hence called producers.

Consumers: Include all animals which depend on producers directly or indirectly for their food.

Division of Consumers

(i) Herbivores: Plant eaters. Example: goat, deer.

(ii) Carnivores: Flash eaters. Example: tiger, crocodile.

(iii) Omnivores: Eats both plants and animals. Example: human.

(iv) Parasites: Live on the body of host and take food from it. Example: lice, Cuscuta.

Decomposers: Include organisms that decompose the dead plants and animals. Example: bacteria, fungi. These help in the replenishment of natural resources.

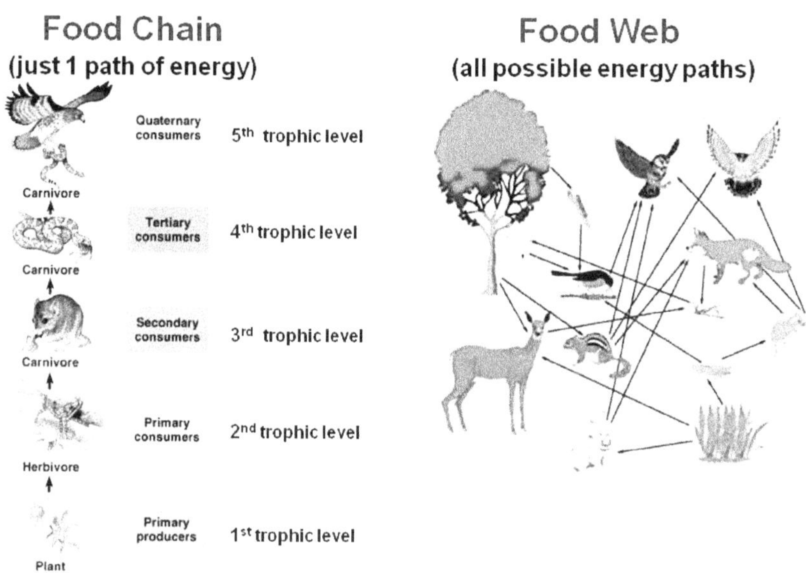

FOOD CHAIN

Ozone layer

Ozone layer is a protective blanket around the earth which absorbs most of the harmful UV (ultraviolet) radiations of the sunlight, thus protecting living beings from many health hazards such as skin cancer, cataract, destruction of plants etc. Ozone (O3) layer is present at higher levels of atmosphere (i.e. stratosphere). It is a deadly poison at ground level.

Formation of ozone molecule

(i) The high energy UV radiations break down the O2 molecules into free oxygen (O) atoms.

O →(UV) O + O (atoms)

(ii) These oxygen atoms then combine with oxygen (O2) molecule to form the ozone molecule.

O2 + O → O3 (ozone)

Depletion of ozone layer

The decrease in the thickness of ozone layer over Antarctica was first observed in 1985 and was termed as ozone hole.

This decrease was linked to excessive use of synthetic chemicals like chlorofluorocarbons (CFCs) which are used in refrigerators, ACs, fire-extinguishers, aerosols sprays etc.

United Nations Environment Programme (UNEP) succeeded in forging an agreement to stop CFC production at 1986 levels (KYOTO PROTOCOL) by all countries

Types of materials in Garbage

(i) Biodegradable: Substances which can be decomposed by the action of microorganisms are called biodegradable wastes.

Example: fruit and vegetable peels, cotton, jute, dung, paper, etc.

(ii) Non-biodegradable wastes: Substances which cannot be decomposed by the action of micro-organisms are called non-biodegradable wastes. Example: plastic, polythenes, metals, synthetic fibres, radioactive wastes, pesticides etc.

Micro-organisms release enzymes which decompose the materials but these enzymes are specific in their action that's why enzymes cannot decompose all the materials.

Methods of waste disposal

(i) **Biogas plant:** Biodegradable waste can be used in biogas plant to produce biogas and manure.

(ii) **Sewage treatment plant**: The drain water can be cleaned in sewage treatment plant before adding it to rivers.

(iii) **Land fillings:** The wastes are buried in low lying areas and are compacted by rolling with bulldozers.

(iv) **Composting:** Organic wastes are filled in a compost pit and covered with a layer of soil, after about three months garbage changes to manure.

(v) **Recycling:** Non-biodegradable wastes are recycled to make new items.

(vi) **Reuse**: It is a conventional technique to use an item again. Example: newspaper for making envelops.

MOST IMPORTANT QUESTIONS

Q1. Which of the following is biodegradable?

(a) Plastic mugs (b) Leather belts (c) Silver foil (d) Iron nails

Q2. Which of the following is a logical sequence of food chain

(a) producer → consumer → decomposer

(b) producer → decomposer → consumer

(c) consumer → producer → decomposer

(d) decomposeràproducer → consumer

Q3. An ecosystem includes [NCERT Exemplar Problems]
(a) all living organisms
(b) non-living objects
(c) both living organisms and non-living objects
(d) sometimes living organisms and sometimes non-living objects

Q4. Which group of organisms are not constituents of a food chain? [NCERT Exemplar Problems]
(a) Grass, lion, rabbit (b) Plankton, man, fish, grasshopper
(c) Wolf, grass, snake, tiger (d) Frog, snake, eagle, grass, grasshopper

Q5. Acid rain is caused by the oxides of
(a) carbon (b) nitrogen only (c) sulphur only (d) sulphur and nitrogen

Q6. Which of the two in the following sets belong to the same trophic level?
(a) Grass; Grasshopper (b) Goat; Spider
(c) Hawk ; Rat (d) Frog ; Lizard

Q7. In a food chain, the third trophic level is always occupied by
(a) herbivore (b) carnivore (c) decomposer (d) producer

Q8. The second trophic level is always of-
(a) herbivores (b) autotrophs (c) carnivores (c) producers

Q9. The decomposers in an ecosystem-
(a) convert organic material to inorganic forms
(b) convert inorganic material to simpler forms
(c) convert inorganic material into organic compound
(d) do not break down organic compound

Q10. Which of the following is an abiotic component of an ecosystem?
(a) Humus (b) Bacteria (c) Plants (d) Fungi

Q11. Which of the following is not a terrestrial ecosystem-
(a) forest (b) desert
(c) aquarium (d) grassland

Q12. Which of the following is biodegradable?
(a) Plastic mugs (b) Leather belts
(c) Silver foil (d) Iron nails

Q13. Which of the following is an autotroph?
(a) Lion (b) Insect (c) Tree (d) Mushroom

Q14. Which of the following is a logical sequence of food chain
(a) producer → consumer → decomposer
(b) producer → decomposer → consumer
(c) consumer → producer → decomposer

(d) decomposer → producer → consumer

Q15. Ozone layer is damaged by-

(a) methane (b) carbon-dioxide

(c) Sulphur-dioxide (d) CFCs

Q16. Fill in the Blanks

1. Those waste materials which can be broken down to non-poisonous substances in nature in due course of time by the action of micro-organisms are called .... wastes.

2. The waste materials which can not be broken down into harmless substances in nature are called ....

3. .... is the ultimate source of energy.

4. In 1987 .... succeeded in forging an agreement to freeze CFC production at 1986 levels.

5. Ozone at the higher levels of atmosphere is a product of UV radiation acting on .... molecule.

6. .... can be classified as herbivores, carnivores, omnivores and parasites.

Q17. Why bacteria and fungi are called decomposers? List any two advantages of decomposers to the environment. [Delhi]

Q18. How is ozone formed in the upper atmosphere? Why is the damage of ozone layer a cause of concern to us? State a cause of this damage. [Delhi(C)]

Q19. "Damage to the ozone layer is a cause for concern." Justify this statement. Suggest any two steps to limit this damage. ' [Delhi]

Answers:

1	2	3	4	5	6	7	8	9	10	11	12	13	14	15
B	A	C	C	C	D	B	A	A	A	C	B	C	A	D

Ans 16. 1. biodegradable

2. non-biodegradable wastes

3. Sun

4. United Nations Environment Programme (UNEP)

5. oxygen (O_2)

6. Consumers

Ans 17. Bacteria and fungi break down the dead remains and waste products of organisms. These microorganisms are called decomposers as they break down the complex organic substances into simple inorganic substances that go into the soil and are used up once more by the plants. Two advantages of decomposers to the environment are as follows:

1. Decomposers feed, on the dead bodies of plants and animals. They return the simple components to soil and help in making the steady-state of the ecosystem by recycling nutrients. They, therefore, create a balance in the environment.
2. They also act as scavengers or cleansing agents of the atmosphere.

Ans 18. Ozone is formed in the upper atmosphere by the reaction of ultraviolet (UV) radiation on oxygen (O_2) molecules. The damage to the ozone layer is a cause of concern to us as due to its damage, more ultraviolet rays reach the earth's surface causing various health hazards.
A cause of this damage is the presence of a large number of chlorofluorocarbons in the atmosphere.

Ans 19. The ozone layer prevents harmful ultraviolet radiation to enter the atmosphere and reaching the earth's surface. Depletion of the ozone layer has become a cause for concern because it can cause serious effects on the human body and other organisms of the environment like fatal diseases such as skin cancer, changes in genetic material DNA, eye damage, etc.
Two steps to limit this damage are as follows:

1. Judicious use of aerosol spray propellants such as fluorocarbon and chlorofluorocarbons which cause depletion or hole in the ozone layer.
2. Control over large scale nuclear explosions and limited use of supersonic planes.

MOST IMPORTANT QUESTIONS

Q1. Inside the magnet, the field lines moves
(a) from north to south (b) from south the north
(c) away from south pole (d) away from north pole

Q2. By which instrument, the presence of magnetic field be determined?
(a) Magnetic Needle (b) Ammeter (c) Galvanometer (d) Voltmeter

Q3. A current through a horizontal power line flows from south to North direction. The direction of magnetic field line 0.5m above it is
(a) North (b) South (c) West (d) East

Q4. A soft iron bar is introduced inside the current carrying solenoid. The magnetic field inside the solenoid
(a) will decrease (b) will remains same
(c) will increase (d) will become zero

Q5. When current is parallel to magnetic field, then force experience by the current carrying conductor placed in uniform magnetic field is
(a) Twice to that when angle is 60° (b) Thrice to that when angle is 60°
(c) zero (d) infinite

Q6. The instrument that use to defect electric current in the circuit is known as
(a) electric motor (b) A.C generator
(c) galvanometer (d) none of the above

Q7. Earth wire carries
(a) current (b) voltage (c) no current (d) heat

Q8. The device used for producing electric current is called
(a) generator (b) galvanometer
(c) ammeter (d) motor

Q9. A D.C generator works on the principle of
(a) ohnis law
(b) Joule's law of heating
(c) faraday's law of electromagnetic induction.
(d) none of the above

Q10. A soft iron bar is introduced inside the current carrying solenoid. The magnetic field inside the solenoid
(a) will decrease (b) will remains same
(c) will increase (d) will become zero

Q11. In the domestic electric circuits, the red coloured insulated copper wire is called
(a) Neutral wire (b) Fuse wire
(c) Live wire (d) Earthing wire

Q12. The factors on which one magnetic field strength produced by current carrying solenoids depends are
(a) Magnitude of current (b) Number of turns
(c) Nature of core material (d) All of the above

Q13. In electric motor, to make the coil rotating continuously in the same direction, current is reversed in the coil after every half rotation by a device called
(a) carbon brush (b) commutator

(c) slip ring (d) armature

Q14. Inside the magnet, the field lines moves

(a) from north to south (b) from south the north

(c) away from south pole (d) away from north pole

Q15. Overloading is due to

(a) Insulation of wire is damaged

(b) fault in the appliances

(c) accidental hike in supply voltage

(d) All of the above

Q16. What is meant by solenoid? How does a current carrying solenoid behave? Give its main use.

Q17. a) Describe activity with labelled diagram to show that a current carrying

conductor experience a force in a magnetic field.

(b) State the rule to determine the direction of force.

Q18. .List in tabular form two major differences between an electric motor and a generator.

Answer:

1	2	3	4	5	6	7	8	9	10	11	12	13	14	15
B	A	A	C	A	C	C	A	C	C	C	D	B	A	D

Ans 16. Solenoid: A coil of many circular turns of insulated copper wire wound on a cylindrical insulating body (i.e., cardboard etc.) such that its length is greater than its diameter is called solenoid.

When current is flowing through the solenoid, the magnetic field line pattern resembles exactly with those of a bar magnet with the fixed polarity, i.e. North and South pole at its ends and it acquires the directive and attractive properties similar to bar magnet. Hence, the current carrying solenoid behave as a bar magnet.

Use of current carrying solenoid: It is used to form a temporary magnet called electromagnet as well as permanent magnet.

Ans 17. (a) Without using a magnet, magnetic field can be produced by flowing the current through a straight conductor or a solenoid.

Aim : To show that magnetic field exerts a force on a current carrying conductor.

Apparatus required : Aluminium rod, stand, strong horse shoe magnet, cell, key and connecting wires.

Procedure :

1. Hang the aluminium rod with the help of clamp stand such that it passes between the North and South pole of the magnet with the magnetic field directed upwards and the rod being horizontal and perpendicular to the field.
2. Connect the aluminium rod in series with a battery, a key as shown in figure.
3. Plug the key, the current flows through the rod from Q to P and observe the direction of motion of the rod.
4. Reverse the direction of current by reversing the battery connection. Again observe the direction of displacement of aluminium rod.
5. Restore the original direction of current and change the direction of field vertically downwards by interchanging the two poles of the magnet. Observe the deflection of rod again.
6. Place the wire parallel to magnetic field and allow the current to pass through it. Check the deflection of rod again.

Observation :

1. On plugging the key in step 3, the aluminium rod moves towards left.
2. In step 4, rod displaces towards right.
3. In step 5, rod moves towards right again.
4. In step 6, rod does not move in any direction.

Conclusion :

1. Magnetic field exerts a force on a current carrying conductor.
2. The force exerted on the current carrying conductor depends upon the direction of current and direction of magnetic field acting on it.
3. Displacement of the rod or the magnetic force on it is largest when the direction of current is at right angle to the direction of magnetic field.
4. When current carrying conductor is placed parallel to the magnetic field, it experiences no force.

   (b) Direction of force experienced by a current carrying straight conductor placed in a magnetic field which is perpendicular to it is given by Fleming's left hand rule.

Stretch the thumb, forefinger and middle finger of left hand in such a way that they are mutually perpendicular to each other. If the forefinger points in the direction of magnetic field and the middle finger in the direction of current, then the thumb will point in the direction of motion or the force acting on the conductor.

Ans 18.

Electric motor	Electric Generator
(*i*) It converts electrical energy into mechanical energy	(*i*) It converts mechanical energy into electrical energy.
(*ii*) It works on the principle of magnetic effect of electric current, i.e. when a current carrying conductor is placed perpendicular to the direction of magnetic field, it experiences a force. The direction of force can be found by using the Fleming's left hand rule.	(*ii*) It is based on the electromagnetic induction, i.e. current can be induced in a coil by moving it in a magnetic field. The direction of induced current can be found by using the Fleming's right hand rule.
(*iii*) Armature is rotated in the magnetic field by supplying electric current to it by some external source such as battery to get the mechanical work.	(*iii*) Armature is rotated in the magnetic field by some external mechanical force to produce electric current.

VIII

Assertion-Reasoning Questions

Assertion-Reasoning Questions

Dear Students, As we Know in assertion-reasoning questions all options are the same. So we give you a direct answer to save papers & trees.

This is a same option for all Assertion-Reasoning Questions

(a) Both A and R are true and R is the correct explanation of A.

(b) Both A and R are true but R is not the correct explanation of A.

(c) A is true but R is false.

(d) A is false but R is true.

Q1. Assertion: Magnesium ribbon burns with a dazzling white flame and changes into a white powder.

Reason: It is formed due to the reaction between magnesium and oxygen present in the air.

Q2. Assertion : The total mass of the elements present in the products of a chemical reaction has to be equal to the total mass of the elements present in the reactants.

Reason : Mass can be created and destroyed in a chemical reaction.

Q3. Assertion: Calcium oxide reacts vigorously with water to produce slaked lime (calcium hydroxide) releasing a large amount of heat.

Reason: Such a reaction in which a single product is formed from two or more reactants is known as a combination reaction.

Q4. Assertion : A dilute ferrous sulphate solution was gradually added to the beaker containing acidified permanganate solution. The light purple colour of the solution.

Reason : $KMNo_4$ is an oxidising agent, it oxidises $FeSo_4$

Q5. Assertion : Chips manufacturers usually use flush bags of chips with a gas such as nitrogen.
Reason : To prevent the oil and fats of the chips from being oxidized.

Q6. Assertion : 1.2 g of silver chloride is taken in a china dish and the china dish is placed in sunlight for sometime.
Reason : To increase the weight it is done.

Q6. Assertion : Some bubbles of gas are seen when a lead is reacted with dilute hydrochloric acid.
Reason : Lead lies above hydrogen in reactivity series.

Q7. Assertion : Some bubbles of gas are seen when a lead is reacted with dilute hydrochloric acid.
Reason : Lead lies above hydrogen in reactivity series.

Q8. Assertion: Baking Powder is used in making cake instead of using only baking soda.
Reason: Baking powder contains tartaric acid which reacts with sodium carbonate and removes bitter taste.

Q9. Assertion: Plaster of Paris is stored in a moisture-proof container.
Reason: Plaster of Paris sets into a hard mass on wetting with water to form anhydrous calcium sulphate.

Q10. Assertion : Copper sulphate crystals are wet because it contains water of crystallisation.
Reason : Water of crystallisation is the fixed number of molecules of water present in one formula unit of salt.

Q11. Assertion : Indicators are used to indicate the presence of acids and bases.
Reason: Methyl orange shows yellow colour for bases.

Q12 Assertion (A) When zinc is added to dilute hydrochloric acid, hydrogen is given off.
Reason (R): Hydrogen chloride molecules contain hydrochloric acid and hydrogen atoms.

Q13. Assertion (A) : Ammonia solution is an alkali.
Reason (R): Ammonia solution turns blue litmus paper red.

Q14. Assertion (A): Baking soda creates acidity in the stomach.
Reason (R): Baking soda is alkaline. Which of the following statement is correct?

Q15. Assertion (A): Plaster of Paris is used by doctors by setting fractured bones.

Reason (R): When plaster of paris is mixed with water and applied around the fractured limbs, it sets into a hard mass.

Q16. Assertion : Bronze is an alloy of Copper and Tin.
Reason : Alloys are a heterogeneous mixture of metals with other metals and non-metals.

Q17. Assertion : Magnesium Chloride is an ionic compound.
Reason: Metals and non-metals react by mutual transfer of electrons.

Q18. Assertion : Zinc can easily displace copper on reacting with a solution of copper sulphate.
Reason(R) : Copper is more reactive metal than zinc.

Q19. Assertion : Zinc oxide is amphoteric in nature.
Reason(R): Zinc oxide reacts with both acids and bases

Q20. Assertion : A mineral is called ore, when metal is extracted from it conveniently and economically.
Reason : All ores are minerals but all minerals are not ores.

Q21. Assertion : Electrical wires can be made by copper.
Reason: Copper is a bad conductor of electricity.

Q22. Assertion : Copper sulphate can be stored in zinc vessel.
Reason: Zinc is less reactive than copper.

Q23. Assertion: Growth hormone stimulates the growth of different body parts
Reason: Gonadotropins stimulate the production of sex hormones

Q24. Assertion: Spores are unicellular bodies.
Reason: In sexual reproduction both male and female sexes are needed to produce new generation.

Q25. Assertion (A) :Human heart is four chambered
Reason : Reason (R) :Vena cava is the only artery that supplies deoxygenated blood to the heart.

Answers:

Ans 1. (a) Both A and R are true and R is the correct explanation of A.

Ans 2. (c) A is true but R is false.

Ans 3. (b) Both A and R are true but R is not the correct explanation of A.

Ans 4. (a) Both A and R are true and R is the correct explanation of A.

Ans 5. (a) Both A and R are true and R is the correct explanation of A.

Ans 6. (c) A is true but R is false.

Ans 7. (a) Both A and R are true and R is the correct explanation of A.

Ans 8. (a) Both A and R are true and R is the correct explanation of A

Ans 9. (c) A is true but R is false.
Ans 10. (d) A is false but R is true.
Ans 11. (b) Both A and R are true but R is not the correct explanation of A.
Ans 12. (b) Both A and R are true but R is not the correct explanation of A.
Ans 13. (c) A is true but R is false.
Ans 14. (d) A is false but R is true.
Ans 15. (a) Both A and R are true and R is the correct explanation of A
Ans 16. (c) A is true but R is false.
Ans 17. (a) Both A and R are true and R is the correct explanation of A
Ans 18. (c) A is true but R is false.
Ans 19. (a) Both A and R are true and R is the correct explanation of A
Ans 20. (a) Both A and R are true and R is the correct explanation of A
Ans 21. (c) A is true but R is false.
Ans 22. (d) A is false but R is true
Ans 23. (b) Both A and R are true but R is not the correct explanation of A.
Ans 24. (b) Both A and R are true but R is not the correct explanation of A.
Ans 25. (c) A is true but R is false.

About Author

<u>Born to Teach</u>

"Destined to be an educator, Concept Classes is known for their natural ability to explain abstract concepts in engaging, interesting and thoughts."

Aadil Khan (M.Tech, B.Tech, NTSA, and Linux Administrator) is an Owner of Concept Classes, Jaipur (Raj.). Concept Classes institute, which was first published on date 01/06/2018 in Ministry of Micro, Small & medium enterprises (MSME, Govt. Of India), Under UAN- RJ32D0003863.

Teaching Experience - 10 years (Including 4 years in Kendriya Vidyalaya & Lecturer in Engineering College). The author's main aim is to clear the basic concept or base of Science & Math's. And Concept Classes Succeed in this AIM as Concept Classes Results tell us.

www.ingramcontent.com/pod-product-compliance
Ingram Content Group UK Ltd.
Pitfield, Milton Keynes, MK11 3LW, UK
UKHW021918190726
13853UKWH00002B/739

9 798885 697965